a leader's
life purpose

CALLING AND DESTINY DISCOVERY TOOLS FOR CHRISTIAN LIFE COACHING

WORKBOOK

TONY STOLTZFUS

To order copies of this book
and other coaching
materials, visit
www.Coach22.com
or phone 757-427-1645.

Table of Contents

Self-Study Schedule and Exercise List

Use this schedule to study through the *Workbook* on your own or with a group. Each chapter is a lesson—you may want to try doing one or two a week. Simply read the chapter and then work through the one to three Core Exercises in the left column. The "Optional Exercises" column on the right offers additional discovery approaches (if you get stuck on a core exercise, try one of these), plus ways to go deeper and learn more in that area.

Lesson	Core Exercises	Optional Exercises	Pg.
Chapter 1-2		*1.1 Coaching Baseline Assessment*	10
	2.1: Jesus' Teaching on Eternal Rewards		24
	2.2: Structuring for Eternal Rewards		25
		3.1 Coaching Bible Studies (on-line)	
Chapter 3-4	4.1: Allegiance Checkup		35
		4.2: Needs, Losses and Bonds	36
		4.3: Clarifying Your Allegiance	37
Chapter 5	5.1: Strengths Inventory		44
	5.2: Strengths Examples (Worksheet)		45
		5.3: Strengths Behind Successes	46
		5.4: Strengths Validation	47
	5.5: Identifying Weaknesses		48
		5.6: Strengths, Type and Energy	49
Chapter 6	DiSC™ Personality Assessment (on-line)		
	6.1: Peer Validation		53
		6.2: Type Night	54
		6.3: My Ideal Team	55
Chapter 7	7.1: Passion Bull's Eye		59
	7.2: Energy Activities		60
Chapter 8	8.1: Big Dreams/Fun Dreams Inventory		67
	8.2: Life Wheel Categories		69
		8.3: Dream Lifestyle	70
		8.4: Envisioning Your Dream	71
	8.5: Dream Themes		72
Chapter 9	9.1: Identifying Obstacles		77
		9.2: Regrets	78

Chapter 1: Introduction to Life Purpose

"When you start out on the journey you think it is all about taking in experiences to fulfill yourself. But it's not. The greatest experience is changing someone else's experience of life. And once you come to that realization, it becomes your foundation, the ace in your pocket, who you are... When you see the world through the lens of others, that's when you find yourself."

Andre Agassi, tennis champion, in *Sports Illustrated*

A committed young missionary came to me for help figuring out his life purpose. Over the weeks we'd been working together he'd poured out his heart to me. We talked about his dreams for starting a ministry center as well as the disappointment of losing his support, his relational challenges with other missionaries, the passion he had for reaching youth and the times he'd chafed under controlling leaders. "So," I finally offered, "Let me sum up our conversation. I'm hearing that you really feel called to ministry; you just don't want to get hurt anymore."

"Yeah, that's about it," he replied.

After a moment's reflection, I asked, "Think about Jesus' life for a second. He was betrayed by one of His inner circle, abandoned by His best friends and tortured to death in the process of living out His life purpose. How will you become like Him if you never get hurt? And how will you ever really know Him if your life is nothing like His?" That rocked him back a bit.

We reflected together on the story of Jesus' life, pondering how the fellowship of His sufferings is inextricably linked with the power of His resurrection. That conversation transformed this young man's expectations about his vocation.

Most life purpose tools are designed to help you look at who you are, discover your wonderful design, deepest passions and innate abilities, and then pursue them. That can be a very profitable and exciting journey, as far as it goes. However, I don't think that kind of process would ever have led Jesus to His agonizing choice in the Garden, where He groaned, "If there is any way to get out of this awful death, that's what I want. But this isn't about me: I'm going to do what *you* want no matter what." Most life purpose tools simply cannot stretch far enough to fit a life like Jesus'. And if the way we do destiny discovery doesn't work with Jesus' life, then something is missing.

I believe that missing piece is "Calling": *an external commission **from** God **for** the sake of others.* Since it is an "external commission," it's found by revelation, not by looking inside. Since it is "for others," it leads us beyond a focus on fulfillment or happiness for ourselves, at least in this life. And it rests on the foundation of Allegiance: you answer a call from God because you have pledged your life to His service. The concepts of Calling and Allegiance give us a way to integrate biblical ideas like suffering and sacrifice into life purpose—ideas that are missing from most popular approaches.

> *Calling is an External Commission from God for the sake of others.*

As Christians, our purpose is woven into the fabric of God's plan for all of creation. Calling is what places us within the context of this larger story. So a balanced, biblical approach to destiny discovery looks in four directions:

- **Outward** at what God reveals *to* us (the external *Call*).
- **Inward** at what our *Design* reveals within us.
- **Backward** at how He has purposefully *Prepared* us through our life experiences.
- **Forward** at the dreams and *Passions* that draw us to our future destiny.

Walking through that kind of process is what this *Workbook* is about. These discovery tools will help you work through all four of these areas and end up with a set of values, a life mission, a life vision, an understanding of your personality type and strengths, and more.

How to Use this Book

You can go through this book on your own, with a peer partner (even better), or with a life coach (the best). Life coaches are trained destiny discovery experts—their encouragement, perspective and grasp of these tools will help you get the most out of this process.

A *Self-Study Schedule* is provided on pages 4-5 to guide you through the discovery process. Each week you read a chapter and then do the two or three core exercises (in the second column) for that area. If you do one section a week, the whole process takes 15 weeks. Or you can do two a week and finish in eight weeks.

The exercises in the third column are optional: if one of the core exercises isn't working for you (or want to go deeper in that area), these provide additional options. All of the exercises reside at the end of the chapters, and are numbered *chapter.x*. So exercise 12.1 is at the end of chapter 12. If you'd like to create a baseline for yourself so you can look back at the end of the process and see how far you have come, take half an hour or so and do the *Baseline Assessment* (exercise 1.1).

Companion Volumes

There are two companion volumes to this *Workbook*. A *Leader's Life Purpose Handbook* is an in-depth guide to coaching others through the life purpose discovery process. It includes all the exercises in this *Workbook*, with added coaching tips, background information and completed examples. It also offers a wealth of coaching principles and techniques illustrated with dialogues and stories from real coaching situations—in total, about two-and-a-half times as much content as in this *Workbook*.

The second companion book is *The Calling Journey,* also by Tony Stoltzfus (due out in the fall of 2009). This book focuses on the developmental process of calling. Based on in-depth studies of biblical and contemporary leaders, *The Calling Journey* presents a five-stage model of calling development and shows you how to create a personal calling time line. Each stage has unique tasks and challenges, so understanding how God deals with leaders in a particular season can make a huge difference in whether you see your circumstances as Preparation or frustration. A shorter presentation of this material is available on the *Stages of Calling Development* CD from Coach22.com.

The Great Adventure

God has uniquely *Designed* you to display a special facet of His character in your being, and to put it into action through your doing. He has gifted you with unique *Passions* to motivate you to serve, provided a lifetime of *Preparation* experiences, and *Called* you to a life mission that provides real joy as a by-product of giving your life to His larger purposes. God has a great purpose for you. So take up the challenge to discover and live your unique destiny! Your greatest adventure is your greatest service to your King.

Design Baseline Assessment  **1.1a**

The questions below give us a baseline for creating a life purpose discovery plan. Take five to eight minutes to complete this page. If you don't know what to say on a question, or would have to dream up an answer on the spot, leave that question blank. This isn't a test where you try to get the right answers. We're trying to ascertain what you already know for sure about your life purpose so we know where to start.

1. What is your personality type (DiSC™, Myers-Briggs© or other assessment)?

2. List several key characteristics associated with that personality type.

3. List the types of three family members or co-workers (if you know them). After each, give an example of how your personality type complements or conflicts with theirs.

4. Do you know your spiritual gifts? If so, what are your two top ones?

5. Name four in-born talents, abilities or strengths. What are you naturally very good at?

6. Name three weaknesses (places where you *aren't* naturally talented).

7. What percentage of the time does your job allow you to function in your best strengths?

The questions below give us a baseline for creating a life purpose discovery plan. Take five to eight minutes to complete this page. If you don't know what to say on a question, or would have to dream up an answer on the spot, leave that question blank. This isn't a test where you try to get the right answers. We're trying to ascertain what you already know for sure about your life purpose so we know where to start.

1. What is your core passion in life?

2. Have you ever made a list of life dreams? Name two or three dreams either from that list or ones you'd put on it if you had one.

3. What are two areas of your current role that energize you, and two things that drain you? Were those easy or difficult to think of?

4. Have you ever written out a set of personal or leadership values? If so, state two below.

5. How well does your primary role align with your core passions and what energizes you? What would need to change to make it a great fit?

The questions below give us a baseline for creating a life purpose discovery plan. Take five to eight minutes to complete this page. If you don't know what to say on a question, or would have to dream up an answer on the spot, leave that question blank. This isn't a test where you try to get the right answers. We're trying to ascertain what you already know for sure about your life purpose so we know where to start.

1. List two character qualities you'll need in your destiny role that life has taught you along the way, and say how they connect with your destiny.

2. What are three skills that you've picked up along the way in life that will be vital to fulfilling your call?

3. Give an example of a difficult experience you've gone through in the last few years that you are consciously aware has specifically prepared you for your destiny.

4. Name a past event where you felt you were doing what you were born to do, and two things that event tells you about your life purpose.

The questions below give us a baseline for creating a life purpose discovery plan. Take five to eight minutes to complete this page. If you don't know what to say on a question, or would have to dream up an answer on the spot, leave that question blank. This isn't a test where you try to get the right answers. We're trying to ascertain what you already know for sure about your life purpose so we know where to start.

1. What has God revealed to you about your calling in life?

2. To what degree do you feel you are on-course with what God has called you to? How do you know that?

3. Describe one of your life messages: a message for the world God has uniquely incarnated in you in a place He has deeply dealt with you.

4. Describe specifically the people you are called to serve or the need you are called to meet.

5. What is your life mission? (The task(s) you must complete in life.) What role will you ultimately be in, and how does it fit your design and help you fulfill that mission?

Chapter 2: The On-Purpose Life

"When I'm focused, there is not one single thing, person, anything that can stand in the way of my doing something. There is not. If I want something bad enough, I feel I'm gonna get there."

Michael Phelps, Olympic Swimmer, in *Sports Illustrated*

Michael Phelps, the winner of eight gold medals at the 2008 Olympics, was in a pool before his first birthday. His older sisters swam competitively (one came heartbreakingly close to making the Olympic team), and as he followed in their footsteps he developed both a love for swimming and a fierce competitive desire. At only 11, Coach Bob Bowman recognized him as a rare talent. Besides his swimmer's physique (large hands and feet, abnormally large wingspan, double-jointed ankles, and an eventual height of 6'4"), the youngster had a capacity for hard work and preternatural calm under pressure that gave him tremendous potential.

Phelps identified something he was made to do early in life, and gave himself completely to it (at one point practicing five hours a day every day for five years straight). By pursuing his Olympic dream he raked in millions in endorsements, attained worldwide recognition and became the most decorated swimmer in Olympic history.

The other day I saw an interview of him talking about his new book, No Limits. The host acknowledged Phelps' incredible practice regimen and discipline, then asked a question that cuts to the heart of the idea of destiny: was what he had done possible for others? Or was it something he was uniquely gifted for; that not everyone, even if they gave a maximum effort, could do?

Phelps responded in keeping with his book's title. "I think it's possible... If anyone puts their mind to it and they want it that bad, anything is possible."

The search for purpose in life is as old as humanity itself. In some of His first words to mankind, God gave Adam and Eve a life mission: "Be fruitful and multiply, and fill the earth, and subdue it..." (Gen. 1:22). Our sense of having a destiny is rooted in the way we were made. We all instinctively yearn to do and be something, to make our lives count, to stand before our Creator and hear the words, "Well done" pronounced over our lives. Even before the fall, we were made to work, to steward and to shape our world.

When our basic life needs are met, at some point we all turn toward the bigger questions. Who am I? Where can I find joy and fulfillment in life? What is my purpose? What does God want me to do with what He's given me?

This instinct to search for meaning reveals an important truth: purpose is something that must be *discovered*. God has a unique design for your life, and you must find and follow it. You are made for something—to embody Jesus in a one-of-a-kind way to this world through a life mission. That's your destiny. Co-laboring with God on this journey of joy, sacrifice and service is where you will find meaning in life.

Life Purpose is something that must be discovered and then aligned with.

And once discovered purpose is something you *align* your life with. Knowing what you are supposed to do with your life isn't worth a whole lot unless you actually do it. That's hard work. Realignment means changing habits, taking risks and sacrificing the good to get the best. That's why people who are asking the big questions often look to a life coach for the tools, perspective and process to help them live with clarity of purpose.

Cultural vs. Biblical

Our culture has its own answers to the big questions of meaning and fulfillment. In recent years, the concept of life purpose has become a powerful theme in the American psyche—as Phelps' book shows. We've adopted the belief that everyone has a life purpose, that your purpose is within your reach, and that finding and following it leads to a satisfying, significant life. If you find your destiny and give yourself to it, you can be a gold medal winner like Phelps. It's an extension of the original American dream—that this is a land of opportunity where anyone who works hard can "make it," regardless of their social or economic background. Life purpose expands this ideal of the Good Life beyond financial and social success to offer significance and personal fulfillment as well. It is life and liberty with an extra helping of the pursuit of happiness.

Since we live within this culture, our cultural and biblical ideas tend to get mixed together. So we need to do a little sorting out of our underlying philosophy of life purpose before we begin the journey of discovering it.

There is much for Christians to celebrate in how the idea of purpose has penetrated our culture. The idea that we are one-of-a-kind and have a unique contribution to make ups the value of human life. Believing that destiny is for everyone and not just a chosen few great leaders is a vital bulwark against controlling or authoritarian leadership. That one's destiny can be found and followed inspires us to leave a legacy for others instead of just trudging through life in survival mode.

The idea of destiny also leads inexorably toward a Creator—otherwise, where does this destiny we have built into us come from? Destiny means we are made for something; that life is unfolding according to a plan. But there can only be a plan if there is a Planner.

Having the freedom to dream up your own destiny sounds fun, but it ultimately leaves you empty. If there is no God and no afterlife, your destiny dies with you. A destiny that doesn't make you part of some larger, lasting purpose loses much of its significance. So seeking for meaning is ultimately seeking for God—and having a society of seekers is a great advantage in reaching people for Christ.

Society's new focus on life purpose also signals a change in our definition of success. In the past, money, power and reputation were the measuring sticks. But now success is also about doing what gives you satisfaction, joy and significance. Many still live as if wealth and fame is the path to the good life, but more and more people are leaving behind these old idols. Some search for significance in causes like saving the planet or working for good government, while others focus on relationships instead of accomplishments, and still others abandon both social and career ambition to live simpler lives. This also is a great opportunity for Christianity—pursuing significance in life seems much more likely to lead to God than running after money or power.

Testing Our Picture of Purpose

However, the new life purpose ideal also makes assertions believers need to test. For instance, Michael Phelps repeats the oft-stated view that we can do anything we dream of. There are no limits to human accomplishment. But I beg to differ with Phelps—I'm five-foot-nine, with short arms and small hands, and no amount of extraordinary effort could *ever* have made me into an Olympic-caliber swimmer! The "no limits" idea simply doesn't work in real life. God never says that we can be and do anything. But when we fully embrace His design for us and grow into exactly what He created us to be, we'll really be living.

Another life purpose tenet we should examine closely is the view that living this healthy, wealthy, culturally-defined Good Life is something God promises us. In ministry circles this ideal is often expressed as "the believer's birthright"—that Christians who operate in the realm of faith can appropriate all the promises of God who has designed us to live a wonderful, wealthy, happy, trouble-free Good Life.

But is this really true? Another good check of a purpose principle is to see if it works in the real lives recorded in the Bible. Does the believer's birthright theology match with what we know actually took place in the life of, say, Paul? If the writer of half the New Testament was afflicted with things like shipwreck, beatings, hunger, imprisonment and sleepless nights, then maybe we need to rethink the idea that happiness, wealth, health and freedom is every believer's birthright.

A third concept that bears reexamination is that achieving a life task is within anyone's grasp. Some say that if you really lay hold of God and live obediently you will certainly complete your mission in life. We might test this by asking, "Does this idea hold true in every culture and at every time in history, or is it unique to 21st century North America?" Think about the believers under persecution in first century Rome, or those killed in the ethnic cleansing in Rwanda, or the pastors in China who've been imprisoned for their faith. In what sense are or aren't they fulfilling their life mission?

This brings to mind a committed, lifetime missionary friend who died suddenly of a heart attack in his forties. He left two kids and a wife behind—I doubt that on the day of his death he was celebrating the completion of his life's work.

We live in a dangerous world, and no one knows how many days he has left. Wars, persecution, disease, financial turmoil and even other people can interfere with the best laid plans. Your dream may be to kick the winning field goal at the Super Bowl—but there are 11 guys on the other side of the line of scrimmage whose dream is to block it! What you can do is fully live *toward* what you were made to do in each moment you are given, and become the person you are called to be. Will you live to see the completion of your life mission? That's in the hands of God.

Your Purpose within God's Purposes

Since being made for something means there is a Maker, the starting point for understanding life purpose is grasping God's overall purposes for humanity. In Ephesians 2:7, Paul states that his purpose is "to show the immeasurable riches of his grace in kindness toward us in Christ Jesus." God's fundamental intention for the universe is simply to love us. We are at the center of His purpose because we are at the center of His love.

Love is not about you: it is about the object of your love. God is not focused on what He can get out of His relationship with us. He isn't trying to win our loyalty, He doesn't need our worship, and He's not angling to get something back. He is already full. He does not need. But rather than making Him aloof and disinterested, His already-full-ness is what allows Him to love us with unconditional, immeasurable, overwhelming abandon. It is precisely because God does not need anything from us that He can love us unconditionally.

When Scripture says love "does not seek its own" (I Cor. 13:5) it is describing God Himself. God is love, and God is about love, not about getting what He wants. God is not about Himself. And that is why Jesus is so clear about not living for self: to make it your primary focus to get your own needs met is utterly un-Godlike. How could you understand a God who gives himself totally for us when you are the complete opposite? The only way to have any kind of a mutual relationship with an all-giving God is to learn to give and love freely yourself. Otherwise, the two of you have nothing in common. Living for personal gratification so twists the human heart that it becomes literally impossible to comprehend the heart of God.

Living for personal gratification so twists the human heart that it becomes literally impossible to comprehend the heart of God.

What you focus on and make priority in life is what you love. The first love of American society is things. But you literally cannot love both God and things ("mammon")—because giving your heart to one will make the other incomprehensible.

To put this in practical terms, the core life purpose of a God-centered individual is never about being financially independent, or enjoying your retirement years, or traveling the world, or being successful in your career. Those objectives are small and self-centered—they look inward, toward your wants and needs, while love looks outward, to the wants and needs of others.

Purpose as Becoming

That's why at the most fundamental level, our life purpose involves becoming like Christ, so that we can enter fully into our love relationship with God. We are first called to *be*, to incarnate Christ, and then to *do* out of that being. Our life mission (what we do) is simply the channel for the Christ in our being to come out.

And since God is love, letting him come out in what we do means loving others. That's the heart of every life mission. Only a life focused on loving and serving others meets the standard of looking like Jesus. The amazing thing is that as we focus on giving instead of taking, the temporal blessings of joy, fulfillment and significance come to us even though we are not pursuing them.

> *At the most fundamental level, our life purpose is to become like Christ.*

Seeing the heart of life purpose as an incarnation you become instead of a mission you do can make an enormous difference in the trajectory of your life. For example, my father's dream was to teach at one of our denomination's colleges. He actually had a position there, but couldn't get tenure because he only had a Master's degree. So he left to get his PhD, with the hope that he'd have a long-term job when he came back.

But once he graduated, he had a tough time finding any position at all, let alone within the denomination. The good jobs in his field often had hundreds of applicants, and he ended up taking something that wasn't really what he wanted.

Years later, he again got the chance to land his dream job, this time at his alma mater. He was one of the final two candidates for the position—and then the college decided they needed more gender balance in the department and only offered a one-year contract. He was hurt and frustrated, and withdrew his name. When the position came up again in a year, despite our encouragement, he didn't even apply. My dad felt his life dream was thwarted because he couldn't *do* what he wanted in the place where he envisioned himself. If he had thought of his purpose in *being* terms, he would have realized that he *had* fulfilled it.

The role my dad sought was only a container for his purpose. The true desire of his heart was to communicate his wonder and love of learning about nature to others. The teaching role he thought was his call was merely a vehicle for his heart's desire. But because he mistook the vehicle for the heart of his call, he missed a part of the joy of his destiny that was right there for the taking.

Three Levels of Purpose

The being/doing tension of call gets clearer if we go back to Scripture and break down God's purposes for humanity into some categories. In Ephesians 1 Paul discusses our destiny as God's children. The passage concludes with God's overriding purpose: "to unite all things in Christ; things in heaven and things on earth" (Eph. 1:10; RSV). Paul saw our ultimate aim as *being together* with God in Christ, in the Kingdom of Heaven. All God's other objectives for humanity flow from this primary purpose.

Paul also talks about purpose in terms of a personal life mission he had to fulfill. "To me, the very least of all the saints, this grace was given: to preach to the Gentiles the unfathomable riches of Christ" (Eph. 3:8). This is to be done "in accordance with the eternal purpose which he carried out through Christ Jesus our Lord" (3:11). This connection is crucial. The eternal purpose is the primary, *being together* purpose mentioned above. The

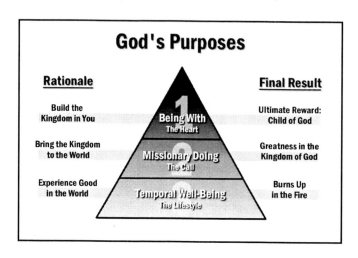

doing purpose of our lives—our life mission—needs to synchronize with the *being together* purpose that is God's ultimate aim.

Here's what that means in practical terms. God's first priority is *you*: to be in a loving relationship with you and to bring you into oneness with Him. The second priority is your life mission. Because His purposes are in this order, *God will sometimes put your life mission on hold to have your heart.* If your life is out of balance because you are doing too much ministry, God will eventually call you back to a balanced life, even if the ministry suffers. Even when you are doing well, living on-purpose and making a difference, God will prune your life back and lead you into outwardly-unproductive wilderness seasons to gain a greater grip on your heart.

A friend of mine is a great example of this principle. Steve owned a 40-million-dollar company and was fully absorbed in running it, to the glory of God as best he understood it at the time. In the process of capturing his heart, God pruned Steve's life way back to prepare for greater growth. His company went bankrupt, he endured a string of legal battles, and finally his home burned down.

These challenges reformed him into a man of prayer, a friend of solitude, and someone with a heart for the nations. He now travels overseas regularly to train leaders and bring businesspeople to Christ. He's expressed to me several times how grateful he is for God's intervention, because he has come to a level of intimacy with God that he never knew before.

Steve learned that when God designs your life, growth in being together takes precedence over productive doing. Our relationship with God grows as we become more like Christ, and are therefore able to understand Him and enter into Him more fully.

There is a third level of purpose as well. God is concerned not just with our *being together* with Him and our *missionary doing* to bring His Kingdom to others, but with our *temporal well-being,* too. "If God so clothes the grass of the field… will he not much more clothe you? … your heavenly Father knows that you need all these things" (Mt. 6:30-32).

God wants you to see good in this life. He wants you to succeed, to experience love and intimacy in relationships. As the Westminster Catechism teaches, "man's chief end is to glorify God and enjoy him forever."

> ## Living the On-Purpose Life
>
> Living on purpose means aligning with the three levels of God's purposes for us:
>
> - **First, Deep Intimacy** with God and others; becoming a person who is full, with a overflowing capacity to love
> - **Second, a Significant Mission** in life; total commitment to be a unique part of God's eternal purposes and leave a legacy behind
> - **Third, Joy in the Journey.** The ability to find contentment in your lot in life based on being rooted in the deeper reality of Christ's love.

However, this isn't God's only (or even primary) purpose for you. Your union with Him and becoming like Christ is much more important. So *God will put your happiness on the back burner to gain more of your heart.* That's right: success in your career, financial security, satisfying relationships, good health, you name it—all these things God may supply or withhold to gain your heart, because they are of incomparably less value than being with Him forever in heaven. The fundamental error of much of the teaching we hear about prosperity and success is that it elevates this third purpose above the first. Yes, God wants to bless your temporal life— *but in proportion with His larger purposes.*

Take success, for example. A common Preparation experience of biblical leaders is demotion. God regularly moves leaders (like David, Joseph and Moses) out of a large, successful role and into a much smaller sphere of influence at certain stages of life in order to shape them inwardly. Moses' case is particularly poignant—from being a big shot in the palace in Egypt, he went to being a shepherd (remember that herdsman were despised by the Egyptians) and a husband. His sphere of influence shrank down to his sheep and his wife Zipporah, whose name aptly means "little sparrow." That's one of those little details that hints at God's sense of humor—Moses the great deliverer reduced to serving one little sparrow.

In his subsequent ministry, Moses' defining characteristic was humility. He immediately turned to God in every difficulty and asked for help and direction. *Moses became that man in the desert.* God put his success on hold to gain his heart, and in the process Moses became the man who could successfully fulfill his true call. Without the humility he learned from serving a little sparrow, Moses would have been a deliverer in the style of the Egyptian power politics he knew—totally unsuitable for creating a nation out of God's chosen people.

Purposes in Balance

However, life is not about focusing on being to the exclusion of all else. I coach many ministry leaders who view level III as unspiritual and not worthy of their time. So they don't have anything in life they do just for the sheer joy of it—no dreams of interesting vacations, no hobbies, no time to just savor God's creation without a ministry agenda. The problem is, *when you don't meet God at all three levels, you don't have a complete picture of who God is.* If the level II mission dominates your life, it reflects a skewed view that God is mostly about getting us to do something for Him.

And that view of God is picked up and imitated by those you lead. If this is you, ask yourself: "If the people I lead were to follow my example instead of what I say—so that everyone I'm leading worked my hours, had my stress level, spent the amount of time I do with my wife and kids, had my exercise and eating habits—if they imitated my lifestyle, how much good would I be doing?"

The Abundant Life

One of the beauties of Christianity is that the important things are very simple. The on-purpose Christian life simply reflects God's purposes: to love God with all your heart, soul, mind and strength (purpose level I), and to love your neighbor (level II) as yourself (level III)—exactly what Jesus said was most important in life.

Think about it: wouldn't the best possible life be the life of *agape*: one with the freedom, power and goodness to offer the gifts of love, right relationship, justice, compassion, and service to everyone you meet, without needing to get something back? Imagine living that way: full instead of needy; free from any craving for security, significance or acceptance; unencumbered by anger and inner wrestlings, with the internal resources to always offer the best to those around you. That would be an overflowing, abundant life!

For Jesus, the way to a life of overflow was not to get more money, control or freedom, but to give up those things and live to serve. "Give and it will be given to you, pressed down, shaken together and running over" (Luke 6:38; RSV). Instead of getting in order to give, you give and find that somehow it comes back to you. Learning to love like Jesus is the path to a life of overflow that fills others—and in the process produces fulfillment within you.

One way to work at creating this kind of life is *structuring for eternal rewards.* The book of Matthew alone records over 40 ways (see exercise 2.1) to choose treasures in heaven over rewards on earth. These examples involve letting go of temporal things for the eternal, going beyond what the world does to model God to others, and forgoing temporal acclaim to gain honor from God.

Structuring for eternal rewards simply means building these principles into your lifestyle so radically that unless heaven is real, your life doesn't make any sense. A while back I worked with a Christian entrepreneur who was reevaluating his life. He had it all—the beautiful home with a pool, great income, complete control over his schedule, and good health. And yet he was considering leaving that dream lifestyle to go plant a church in the inner city. That's crazy—unless you are living for eternal rewards and not for what you can get in the here and now.

Your life today may not require that major a step. But here's a challenge: take the list of eternal rewards in worksheet 2.1 and find one that you can integrate into your life so radically that it breathes the scent of heaven to everyone who touches your life (see exercise 2.2).

Purpose and Suffering

Let's try an experiment. Take a few minutes and visualize fulfilling your destiny in this life. As much as you can, picture that moment of ultimate accomplishment. You might be sitting with a group of students you taught years ago and hearing the difference you made in their lives. Or it could be attaining a certain position, seeing your children mature and successful, planting a thriving church, or graduating with a certain degree. You are there, in that instant. Who is with you? What is the setting? What is the impact you are having on others? Close your eyes and immerse yourself in the details for a bit.

Now, what emotions are you feeling when you visualize reaching your destiny?

When I ask groups this question, I hear words like happiness, fulfillment, peace, thankfulness, accomplishment, or contentment. We tend to see destiny fulfillment as something joyful and satisfying. And those are common emotions in destiny experiences.

But let's look at another example. What do you think Jesus was feeling at the moment when *He* was fulfilling his destiny in this life? Jesus' life call was to take on the sins of the world and die on the cross to offer us life. What did Jesus experience at his penultimate moment?

That little exercise brings a whole new perspective to thinking about purpose. The most obvious thing we can learn from it is that *suffering is a part of purpose.* I've always been intrigued by the list of lives of the faithful in Hebrews 11. Paul talks about those who through faith conquered Kingdoms, stopped the mouth of lions, escaped the sword, or won their dead back by having them resurrected. Sounds really good so far! And then, without even pausing for breath, Paul goes on to talk about those who were tortured, stoned, sawn in two, destitute, afflicted, poorly treated, who never got the honor they deserved—and he attributes to both groups the same faith! These are all people who lived their destiny.

Paul is saying that a Christian's life purpose may as easily lead to great temporal suffering and loss as to great deeds and great gain. This isn't very attractive at first glance! But viewing suffering as a part of life is actually very powerful. If suffering is included in God's plan, then God works through it, and the Planner still has things in hand. He may even bring us gifts in suffering that empower us to fulfill our destiny. If, on the other hand, we aren't supposed to suffer, then anything bad that happens to us simply indicates that we are off course.

Jesus' life powerfully affirms that suffering has great purpose. Therefore, all of life, good and bad, has purpose. God is at work in *everything.* He'll take whatever is going on in your life and leverage it to build you into the image of Christ, if you engage it with a sense of purpose (Rom. 8:28). The objective of living on purpose is not to eliminate adversity (which is impossible anyway), but to meet God in it. True Kingdom greatness is always only a moment away—the time it takes you to say, "OK God: how do you want to meet me in this?" The most transformational, important things we learn in life we usually learn the hard way.

This leads to another important life purpose truth: *your call is often discovered within your own sufferings or the sufferings of others.* For example, everyone who goes on a short-term mission trip and feels drawn to serve those living in darkness and squalor has found a call within the sufferings of others. Anyone who grew up as a social misfit and determines to reach those on the fringes of society, or was a child of divorce and finds a call in fostering healthy marriages, or who grieved her own miscarriage and ends up working with mothers who miscarry, has found destiny within adversity. The Preparation and Calling sections of this *Workbook* include exercises designed to help you find clues to your purpose within your experiences of suffering.

Kingdom Success

There is one more important life purpose principle I want to highlight in Jesus' destiny story. By almost any popular measure, Jesus' temporal life was a failure. He died young. The last of His clothes were raffled off by the Roman guards. He was unable to support His widowed mother. His teaching was rejected by the religious authorities, He received a death sentence from His own people, and His small band of followers scattered to the four winds. He left no writings or organizational structure behind. He never traveled farther than 70 miles from His hometown, and was unknown outside of that small corner of the world. From all appearances the new Kingdom Jesus talked about was going to die with Him.

> ### Mis-Understanding the Scriptures
>
> - *"Seek ye first to get the financial inheritance that is your birthright as a child of God, because you deserve for all these things to be added to you."*
>
> - *"For the love of money is the root of all fulfillment; those who never get rich have... pierced their hearts with many pangs."*
>
> - *"Have this mind amongst yourselves, as Christ did, who, though he was in the form of God, did not think that that was enough, so he built a ministry empire, and sought many others to serve his vision, so that every tongue would confess what a great leader he was."*
>
> - *"For none who seek to live godly in Christ will be persecuted or meet any kind of struggle or suffering."*

However, from the perspective of 2000 years later, He's the most influential man who ever lived. Which raises an important question: how do you measure success?

God has a simple success standard. In the Kingdom of God, success in life is about stewardship: making the most of what we have been given. The parable of the talents, for instance (Mt. 25:14-30), teaches us that we are stewards of our lives, and taking good care of God's gift means taking risks and stretching ourselves to use our abilities, rather than letting them lie dormant. The master rewarded the servants who fully used whatever they had been given, and criticized the one who wasted the opportunity. He never compared them with each other; instead comparing their results to the resources they'd been given. The only scale you are measured against is what God has placed in you.

Defining success in terms of stewardship also means we don't need to strive to be something we're not. Life is not a competition: it has nothing to do with being as good as or better than someone else. Jesus was a success because He completed the unique task He was sent to do. Our success comes the same way.

> "Indeed, I count everything as loss because of the surpassing worth of knowing Christ Jesus my Lord. For His sake I have suffered the loss of all things, and count them as refuse, in order that I may gain Christ and be found in him... that I may know him and the power of his resurrection, and share in his sufferings, becoming like him in his death, that if possible I may attain the resurrection of the dead."
>
> Paul, speaking about his life purpose (Phil. 3:7-11; RSV)

In my younger days I remember reading about John Wesley, who preached an average of three sermons a day and is estimated to have traveled over 100,000 miles (on horseback!) in his lifetime to preach the gospel. What a great hero of the faith! I chose Wesley as my internal standard for what it meant to be a radical Christian. If I was really sold out to God, I should pray as much as Wesley, serve with as much energy, and have the same kind of impact.

After several years of condemnation, it finally dawned on me that God never created me to be John Wesley. I didn't have his energy, his personality or his famously-devout upbringing—and I didn't have to. What a relief! I only have the abilities I was born with and the background I was born into, and my assignment is to make the most of that. The only way to equal Wesley is to become as much of what I was uniquely created to be as Wesley did—and only God can really measure that.

Greatness in the Kingdom isn't about doing more than someone else—it's about making the most of what you've been given.

Success is not what most people think it is. There are caring mothers, diligent factory workers and guys who coach little league on Saturdays who will be more greatly acclaimed in the Kingdom of heaven than some of our most famous authors, preachers, and missionaries, because *they were more faithful to steward everything they'd been given for Christ than those who had been given much more.*

Below are 30 examples from the book of Matthew on how to live toward heaven.

1. The sermon on the mount (Mt. 5:1-14) is about pursuing eternal rewards:
   - The poor are blessed in the spirit realm—they get the kingdom of heaven
   - Those who mourn will be comforted
   - The gentle will inherit the earth
   - Those who hunger for righteousness and justice will be satisfied
   - Those who give mercy will get it back
   - The pure in heart will see God as the reward for their purity
   - The peacemakers will be recognized as sons of God
   - The persecuted will get the kingdom of heaven as their reward
   - Those falsely accused because of Christ will get a great reward in heaven

2. Whoever is godly and teaches others to be will be great in heaven. (5:19)
3. If *anything* in your life is keeping you from heaven, rip it out! (5:29)
4. If you only love people who love you back, what's different about that? (5:46)
5. If you befriend only your friends, even the world does that. (5:47)
6. If you act religious to get recognition, don't expect any more reward. (6:1)
7. Give gifts secretly instead of publicly, and God will reward you in heaven. (6:2-4)
8. When you practice self-denial, don't flaunt it—or that's all the reward you'll get. Do it secretly for a heavenly reward. (6:16-18)
9. Don't accumulate stuff on earth—add to your bank account in heaven. (6:20)
10. Don't worry about your basic needs (food, clothing and shelter)—God is aware you need them. Seek the Kingdom and that stuff will fall into place. (6:30-32)
11. Grasp onto life and lose it; but let go of it for Jesus' sake and find it. (10:39)
12. Serve the person on the platform and you'll get the same reward. (10:41)
13. Even acts of service as small as giving a child a drink will be rewarded. (10:42)
14. Stand up for Christ before people and He'll stand up for you before God. (10:32)
15. To follow Christ, you must die to self and walk the road of suffering... Don't gain everything the world offers but lose your soul in the process. (16:25-26)
16. If you want treasure in heaven, give away your possessions and follow me. (19:21)
17. If you've left home, family or business to follow Jesus, you'll get back much more in the life to come. (19:29)
18. The greatest in heaven will be everyone's servant on earth. (23:5-11)
19. If you try to look great, you'll be humbled; greatness comes to the humble. (23:12)
20. If you faithfully steward what you've been given, the master will put you in charge of all His possessions in heaven. (24:45-51)
21. Work hard, take risks and make the most of your life for God, and you'll have a high position in heaven. (25:14-30)
22. How you treat the nobodies in your life is how you're treating Jesus. (25:31-46)

Structuring Life for External Rewards

In the book of Matthew, Jesus gives many examples of what it can look like to structure your life for eternal rewards. Some involve letting go of temporal things for the eternal; some push us to go beyond what the world does to be like God, and some challenge us to forgo acclaim in the here and now to gain honor from God. Thirty of these principles are listed on the previous pages. Use the three reflection questions below to help you think about how to apply them in your life.

1. Which of these examples most challenge me today? What one could I implement in a circumstance or decision I face right now?

2. Which of these messages have I been drawn to throughout my life, and most desire that people see in me? What one step could I take to more compellingly convey this message through my life?

3. Which of these do I feel God calling me to begin doing in secret, just for Him?

Chapter 3: The Life Purpose Model

"I don't know what your destiny will be, but one thing I do know: the ones among you who will be really happy are those who have sought and found how to serve."

Albert Schweitzer

Now that we've looked at the biblical basis of life purpose, let's dive into the practical exercises and techniques coaches use to help people find and follow their God-given destiny. We're going to organize our search with a model called the *Seven Life Purpose Questions*. By structuring around these seven themes, we'll help you understand where the process is going and how the different pieces of the puzzle fit together. The seven questions are:

1. **Whose** am I?
2. **Who** am I?
3. **What** has my whole life prepared me for?
4. **Why** do I desire *this*?
5. **Where** is the Master sending me?
6. **When** will this happen?
7. **How** will I get there?

The first five questions have to do with *discovering* life purpose, while the final two have to do with pursuing it (walking out what you've discovered). We'll first do a quick overview of each question, then dive into finding life purpose clues in each area.

The Meaning of the Seven Questions

The first question—"**Whose** am I?"—deals with where we place our fundamental Allegiance. Who are we living *for*? When we make life choices, our basic allegiance may be to ourselves, to another person (where we've subverted our identity to theirs), to our tribe or nation, or to Jesus as master of our lives. This question asks, "When the chips are down, whom have we chosen to serve? Is this life mine to order for my own pleasure and benefit, or do I owe allegiance to something bigger?" Obviously, this can make a huge difference in the trajectory of our lives. To shorten the question, we'll refer to this area as **Allegiance**.

"**Who** am I?" is the Design question. It covers your inborn nature: characteristics like personality type, gifts, strengths, and talents. At this level, people change slowly over time if at all, so understanding who you are is extremely valuable in

---

Defining Terms

When we talk about life purpose, there are a lot of similar terms floating around and we aren't always clear on what each one means. Here are some definitions:

- **Design:** My innate traits or my nature: strengths, personality type, talents, and natural abilities.

- **Experience:** The learned skills, credentials and other assets I acquire in life that I leverage for my life purpose. The nurture counterpoint to Design's nature.

- **Passion:** The internal energy and motivation I have to pursue something I care deeply about.

- **Calling:** An external commission I accept in order to serve a greater good. (For Christians, Calling is "an external commission *from* God *for* others.")

- **Destiny:** A synonym for life purpose.

- **Life Mission:** The ultimate task that channels my life message. The doing part of call.

This leads us to an overall definition of life purpose:

*A Christian's Life Purpose is the energy of **Passion**, channeled through **Experience** and **Design** in **Allegiance** to a God-given **Calling**.*

---

relationships, career, decision-making and other areas. We'll refer to this area as **Design**.

The other side of the nature/nurture dichotomy is the question, "**What** has my whole life prepared me for?" There are many valuable things you pick up along the way in life that shape your destiny: learned skills, work and life experience, character and self-understanding. Taking stock of who you have become compliments the Design picture. We call this area **Preparation**.

The next question asks, "Why?" It taps into desire, passion and motivation. "**Why** do I desire this? Why is this important enough to give my life to?" Passion is a vital part of living an on-purpose life. To accomplish something extraordinary, you'll need exceptional desire to finish the race. This area covers dreams and desires, what energizes you, and your core values and beliefs. You'll find important life purpose indicators within these **Passions**.

The fifth question is, "**Where** is the Master sending me?" This **Calling** is a commission that comes from outside of you to serve a larger end (it serves others, not you). As a Christian life purpose model, the Seven Questions framework

> *A Christian's Life Purpose is the energy of* Passion, *channeled through* Experience *and* Design *in* Allegiance *to a God-given* Calling.

assumes that a call from God is an integral part of *every* believer's life purpose. In this area you'll explore what God has revealed to you about your life mission, the people and needs you are drawn to serve, the message of your life, and how experiences of suffering and sacrifice integrate with your life purpose.

"**When** will this happen?" is the question of **Timing**. If part of your call is to own a business, it may be that now is the time to launch out, or you could have years of preparation ahead before you do. If you want to learn more about timing, the companion book *The Calling Journey* explores life stage models and patterns of Calling development, and shows how to create Calling time lines that explain how you are moving toward your destiny.

The final question is, "**How** will I get there?" This question moves you into the goals and actions that make your life purpose a lived-out reality. You'll get a lot more done if you have a coach or an accountability partner walking with you as you apply what you are learning about your destiny. The basic coaching tools for this **Implementation** process are laid out in my previous books, *Leadership Coaching* and *Coaching Questions*.

So here are the seven purpose questions, with the name for each area:

1. **Allegiance:** Whose am I?
2. **Design:** Who am I?
3. **Preparation:** What has my whole life prepared me for?
4. **Passion:** Why do I desire *this*?
5. **Calling:** Where is the Master sending me?

6. **Timing:** When will this all come together?

7. **Implementation:** How will I get there?

The purpose diagram shows how these questions fit together. The overall context is *Allegiance*: someone who is sold out to Christ is operating on an altogether different playing field than the person whose allegiance is to self. Within the circle of Allegiance are four overlapping areas we mine for life purpose clues: *Design, Passion, Preparation* and *Calling*. Where these four circles converge is the sweet spot: your *Life Purpose*. These five areas are the focus of the remainder of this *Workbook*.

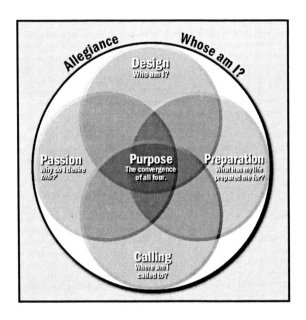

The Life Purpose Play

An excellent analogy for the purpose diagram is acting in a play. When you play a part, you have to get in character and *become* that role in order to complete the task (acting in the play). I like how that incorporates both the being and doing aspects of destiny. Listed below are six guiding principles of our life purpose model, laid out using the play analogy. When these come together, you can put on the performance of your life.

1. **God has created you for a unique part in His purposes in history**
   Life has meaning as part of God's larger story of creation, redemption and uniting all things in Christ. You have a personal part to play in that story.

2. **You were *Designed* for that part from birth in God's foresight**
   You can look inward at your talents, strengths and personality type to find clues to the part that you are fit to play. You were made for this role.

3. **Your *Passion* for your part carries you through**
   There is a fire that burns inside of you to tell this story. Your Passion for the part is what gives you the determination to learn your lines and give your all to the play.

4. **You are *Prepared* for your part through life experience**
   Your whole life to this point is a rehearsal for this ultimate performance. Until you've finished rehearsing, you aren't ready for the opening.

5. **You must follow the script**
   You can be part of God's grand production, or you can do a monologue by yourself on your own stage. In order to be part of God's larger story, you have

to acknowledge **Allegiance** to the director's authority and stick to the script.

6. **The director casts your role**
   You must look *outward* to receive the casting **Call** assigned by the director. You won't fully know the director's purpose for the production until he tells you.

Making Reflection Work for You

I'd like to touch briefly on the topic of reflection before we get started in the discovery process. Adapting how you do the reflection exercises in this book to your unique reflective style and personality type will help you get the most out of them.

One adaptation involves introvert and extrovert learning styles. Introverts discover by getting alone and thinking—their primary drive is to engage something inwardly first, then use it outwardly once they've figured it out. Extroverts think out loud—they learn best by talking. So while introverts do fine with lots individual reflection, the same approach can drive an extrovert crazy. One great way to use your extroversion as an asset is to talk the exercises through out loud with a friend or spouse. Another option for the extrovert is to speak your reflections into a recorder instead of writing them.

Journaling style is another adaptation. When you write down your thoughts, do it in whatever way works for you. Some people journal in complete sentences and paragraphs. Others prefer bullet lists, scrawling in all directions over the page or doodling pictures of their dreams. Some do everything on the computer and don't want to write in the *Workbook* at all. You are free to reflect however works best for you!

Question 1: Whose Am I? (Allegiance)

"Your life is not your own: it belongs to God. To 'be yourself' is to be and do what God wants you to be and do, knowing that God created you for a mission and knows you and your mission better than you do."

Leonard Sweet

Jackie showed up at our door bursting to tell us her news. "Look—I'm engaged!" she exclaimed, proudly holding out the ring on her finger. "We're getting married in June!"

It was one of those moments where it's hard not to let your feelings show. We'd spent several months discipling Jackie as she reoriented her life around the gospel. The big issues were marriage and romantic relationships. Jackie's dream was to get married, and she had fallen in love with the ideal of married life. However, her current boyfriend drank heavily, majored in Nintendo and wasn't a believer. It had been a real struggle for her to realize that this relationship was not compatible with her faith. Two weeks ago she'd finally made the decision to cut ties with him.

"So, come on in and tell us about it," my wife Kathy finally said, rescuing us from an awkward moment. In a few minutes we got the full story. She'd finally mustered up the courage to tell him it was over. The next night he had come over to her apartment, put a knife to his throat and threatened to kill himself if she didn't make up with him—so she did! And now they were engaged.

Kathy asked what God had spoken to her about the decision. Jackie just brushed the question off. "He's the one I want to marry, and that's that."

We didn't see much of Jackie until about a month after the wedding when she came over again to talk. It was a much different conversation this time.

"I just made the biggest mistake of my life," she said soberly, "and now I'm stuck."

When it came to her love life, Jackie's answer to the question, "Whose are you?" was "Mine!" That choice brought her into a painful relationship and great loss. Now that she has come back to the place of choosing allegiance to God in relationships, her pain is being redeemed, and God has even incorporated that redemptive work into her life purpose.

Jackie's story is one of grace and renewal, but it is also one of lost opportunity and rejecting God's purposes. The lesson is that it's impossible to fulfill your destiny as a believer without a fundamental allegiance to the lordship of Christ. Allegiance is the palette you paint your life purpose with. Change the colors, and everything else about the picture of your purpose changes. Unfortunately, Jackie found that out the hard way.

> *It is impossible to fulfill your destiny as a believer without a fundamental allegiance to the lordship of Christ.*

The Pledge of Allegiance

Making Jesus Lord goes beyond trusting Him as savior.[1] It is a one-time decision you make that sets the fundamental direction of your life as one of allegiance to Christ. It is taking your hands off and putting God in charge of everything in your life. A "Pledge of Allegiance" to the Kingdom of God might go something like this:

> *"Jesus, I want you to be in charge of my life. You decide what you want me to do, and I'll do it. I'm inviting you now into every area of my heart and my actions. I choose to keep nothing hidden, under my control or off limits to you. You and I both know I can't even walk this out without your help, so I am asking for that, too. Whenever I hit a place where I can't let go, you have permission to change my heart and make me willing to go there with you."*

Making Jesus Lord doesn't mean that from then on we always do the right thing, or never resist what God intends for us. Otherwise, we'd all be disqualified. The lordship decision means our answer to the question, "Whose am I?" is "Jesus'."

Here's an analogy with a more everyday goal. Let's say that at 16 Holly decides to rise to the maximum level of her abilities and pursue her dream of becoming a soccer player. There is a one-time decision where she sets her heart on being a soccer player (her identity) and doing what it takes to become one. Her decision sets the overall trajectory of her life.

---

1   The early church did not seem to recognize this distinction—you got the whole package at once or nothing at all. Putting the theological questions aside, I think in our day it seems to help people understand lordship to talk about the lordship decision and salvation separately.

Each day contains decisions related to Holly's athletic aspirations. Am I going to run today? How far? Do I have the courage to try out for the varsity? Will I spend my vacation at a soccer camp or hanging out with my friends? Will I believe in my future enough to risk my savings on joining a summer travel team?

Before Holly made the foundational decision to focus on soccer, every choice involved balancing soccer against other priorities in her life and trying to sort out what was most important to her at that moment. But once she made that one dream her life mission, those other choices became much easier. The one-time decision about what was supremely important guided all the lesser decisions about daily priorities.

That kind of "pledge of allegiance" is a good picture of what the lordship decision is like. It is powerful because once made, every other choice to follow God is easier. When believers who have a life pattern of making Jesus Lord realize that God is asking for something, they are able to choose it and move on with life while others are still wrestling with competing voices.

The lordship decision frees up an incredible amount of energy for pursuing God's purpose for your life. Instead of struggling over each small decision, or spending half your time following God and half running away, your heart's inclination pushes you steadily in one direction. Over time, you reach the place where your heart is so set toward God that you have to put forth quite an effort to **not** obey.

You can review where you are at with Allegiance with the *Allegiance Checkup* exercise (4.1) during your devotional time. If you hit some internal resistance, the *Clarifying Allegiance* exercise (4.3) can help you figure out what's going on inside.

Life Purpose for Couples

Keeping your spouse on board is an important part of life purpose discovery. Ideally, couples go through this process together. In marriage, the two shall become one—and hence, their individual destinies are intricately woven together. Working at purpose as partners enriches your experience, provides excellent feedback on your insights, and draws you closer together.

The most common couple-specific life purpose problem is an Allegiance issue: one partner's destiny inappropriately dominates the marriage. In Christian circles, it is common for the husband to assume that his personal call is the priority in the marriage, and to simply fold his wife's energy and abilities into that pursuit, instead of making it a priority to pursue *her* heart and draw out *her* unique destiny.

This pattern violates Paul's most fundamental admonition to husbands: "Husbands love your wives, as Christ loved the church *and gave himself up for her,* to make her holy, cleansing her by washing with water through the word, that he might present her to himself as a radiant church without stain or wrinkle or blemish" (Eph. 5:26-27). The husband is supposed to exhibit sacrificial, *agape* love by giving up his desires and needs for the wife. Unfortunately, the pattern among ministry leaders is often the opposite: the husband expects his wife to give herself up for *his* call. Compared to Christ, who willingly went to His death to secure a future and a hope for His Bride, husbands who don't aggressively pursue, promote and even find ways to defer to their wives' unique callings sorely miss the mark.

I have been deeply touched by leaders I know who have chosen to make room for their spouses' callings and loved them well in this way. A good friend who is a career pastor in his 50's chose his last pastoral position based on where his wife wanted to go to grad school—and then they moved across the country to where *she* got a job. He was very clear before the move that she had sacrificed to put him through grad school and had moved around for his pastoral call, and now it was time for him to step back and sacrifice for her. He ended up substitute teaching in the public schools for two years to help make ends meet until he finally found a ministry position in their community. *That's* laying down your life for your wife!

> ### Are You Unequally Yoked?
>
> Use these questions to evaluate whether one partner's call is inappropriately dominating your marriage:
>
> - Do you know your spouse's life purpose? Can you state it clearly?
> - Has the pursuit of your life mission kept you as spiritual peers, or not?
> - When you've relocated, invested in personal development or sacrificed for one partner's career, how often did one partner benefit?
> - What has your spouse given up for your call? What have you sacrificed for him or her?
> - When you've made major decisions, has one partner often deferred or chosen to simply follow the other?
> - If the primary criteria God judged you under was how you promoted your partner's call, instead of your own, how would you do?

"Hope deferred makes the heart sick" (Prov. 13:12). And I've coached some heartsick spouses over the years. They've deferred, served and sacrificed for decades to advance their spouse's call, but haven't been loved in that same way in return, and there is a hole in their hearts that aches for their husband to pursue them and their life purpose the way he pursues his own. Ignoring your partner's purpose is something that can blow apart a marriage later in life.

An equally important concern is that couples remain true peers in the marriage. Your spouse is made to be the partner at your side—that's where the rib came from (Gen 2:21). However, if one partner aggressively pursues a call and the other doesn't, or if one partner makes the decisions and the other regularly defers (instead of doing the hard work of discerning God's will in the matter), 20 years down the road you'll find that you've ceased to be spiritual peers. Only by *both* pursuing God's call on your lives will your partnership grow to be all that it can be.

Allegiance Checkup

Take these five areas and pray each one during your devotions. Use the words given or expand on them. The idea is to *observe* what goes on in you as you pray, not to try to make yourself into the perfect Christian. Use the reflection questions at the bottom to jot down the thoughts and feelings you experience as you pray. Then simply be present before God with who you are and what you wrote. You are His.

Control

"Lord, run my life. I let go of the reins—I want you to order my life and give me what you think I need. I let go of trying to control my circumstances—I will accept whatever comes from your hand. I let go of controlling the people around me, whether it is through anger or argument or exerting power. I embrace you as my master."

Money

"Lord, I want you to manage all my money, all the time. I will give it, keep it, spend it or save it just as you say. I give you my anxieties about money, too. You are my security and my provider. Thank you for all that I have: it is enough for me. I am content with you and what you've given me: I choose not to look to anything I can buy for my happiness."

Recognition

"Lord, be my reward. Hearing 'well done' from you is the only recognition I choose to work for. I let go of trying to please or impress anyone else so they will like me. I let go of the drive to be famous or accomplished or competent. And I choose to face into conflict and tell the truth, because I trust the outcome to you.

Relationship/Intimacy

"Lord, I trust you with my relationships. You are the protector of my children and the guardian of my heart in friendships. I put you in charge of every area of my marriage (or if I marry). You are the love of my life, and you are enough for me. I won't seek to get my relational needs met my way. My sex life is yours, too—in thought and action, I choose to do things your way and lead a life of purity."

Self-Image

"Lord, I admit that I am a sinner to the core. I utterly die to the need to look like I have it all together—I don't. I let go of needing to be a 'somebody,' of crafting a public image, or of spinning my stories so I look better. I choose to be open about my faults, apologize quickly, and be who I am instead of trying to polish my image. My identity is in your hands."

Reflection

1. How did you experience praying this prayer?
2. Track yourself as you pray through each area. Can you honestly say this? Was it easy or hard? Did it open you to God or make you want to hide?
3. What emotions came to the surface as you prayed? (i.e. joy, fear, relief, anger, etc.) What's behind those feelings?
4. What do these observations tell you about yourself?

When it seems unusually hard to get something done or you struggle to change a behavior, it can be helpful to stop and look for an underlying reason instead of just trying harder. Set some time apart and reflect on the questions below to help identify what's going on under the surface when change is unusually tough.

Needs

- "What do you gain by doing this?"
- "And what does that give you?"
- "What does this pattern (or behavior) give you that you feel you need?"
- "What desire or need drives how you function here?"

Losses

- "What are you afraid will happen if you go there?"
- "What will you lose if this changes?"
- "What are you holding onto or pursuing here that you don't want to lose?"
- "What's the worst case scenario?"

Bonds

- "What memory, desire, fear or drive has a hold on you here?"
- "What are you dealing with that feels bigger or more powerful than you?"
- "What holds you back?"
- "What kind of outside help would give you the best chance of breaking that bond?"

Clarifying Your Allegiance

If you are grappling with pledging allegiance to God in your dreams, life goals or just in daily life, these reflection questions can help you plumb what's going on in you.

God's Touch

- "Where is God asking more of you or bringing something new into your life?"
- "What's God's growth agenda for you right now?"
- "How can you adjust your perspective to better engage this as preparing you for God's purposes for your life instead of as a duty, annoyance or problem?"

Your Heart

- "What fears or hesitancies surface when you think about this new thing?"
- "What draws you on, and where do you hold back?"
- "How does God want to meet you or touch you there?"

Your Sonship

Now, soak for a few moments in the idea that God is 100% for you—you are His dear friend, and He wants nothing except for you to do well, to leave behind the good for the best, and to come up higher with Him. Read the last section of Romans chapter eight where Paul asks, "Who shall separate us from the love of Christ...?" and reflect on these questions:

- "What is God saying to you about His love for you in this area?"
- "How do you want to respond to God's heart?"
- "How do you want to be with God in this endeavor or decision?"

Question 2: Who Am I? (Design)

"The glory of God is a man fully alive."

St. Irenaeus

Saul was between a rock and a hard place again. While his physical attributes garnered attention and opportunity, he'd always battled with fears and insecurities. On the day of his coronation, he'd hidden in the baggage to escape the responsibility of his new role. A few years later, worried sick as his army melted away in the face of the Philistine war machine, he'd stifled his conscience and offered the priestly sacrifice himself in a desperate attempt to keep up morale. Naturally, Samuel showed up just as he was completing the deed. With words that chilled his heart, Samuel announced that Saul's reign would not endure—God had chosen another king for his people. And the Philistine army was still camped right over the next ridge!

Somehow Saul survived that terrible moment, and things appeared to be going well in spite of Samuel's prophecy of doom. He had won victories on every border, and the people acclaimed him for safeguarding their homes and farms. His old mentor had even come back with a commission from God: destroy the Amalekites. Leading a crusade with Samuel's approval restored his popularity, and the recognition and acclaim held back the gnawing fears inside him. Then everything fell apart.

Instead of destroying the spoil, the people wanted to keep their Amalekite treasures. Saul compromised and kept everyone happy. But on the way home from his victory celebration, Saul ran into the prophet—who shredded his self-image by calling out his disobedience and telling him that God had torn away his kingdom.

Saul's old paranoia returned with a vengeance, and this time there was no Samuel, no promise from God and no sense of God's presence to withstand them. Things got so bad that his courtiers suggested recruiting a musician to ease Saul's tormented soul.

In that moment, one of Saul's warriors remembered a young man he'd met named David. "I have seen a son of Jesse the Bethlehemite who is a skillful musician, a mighty man of valor, a warrior, one prudent in speech, and a handsome man; and the Lord is with him" (I Sam. 16:18). So David, youngest son of a poor sheep herder, secretly anointed king by Samuel, was plucked from anonymity, brought to the palace and became part of the king's retinue. He was the epitome of the up-and-coming man. Whenever the evil mood came on Saul, David would play and the king was comforted.

A Tale of Two Callings

I Samuel 16 tells the tale of two intertwined callings. Both men's innate qualities were tied to their roles. Saul's outstanding characteristic was his physical prowess: he was "a choice and handsome man, there was not a more handsome person than he among the sons of Israel; from his shoulders and up he was taller than any of the people" (I Sam. 9:2) Saul was a man of action: early in his kingship he exhibited the personality traits of a dominant leader who could think strategically, rally people to a vision, and get things done (see I Samuel 11). In other words, Saul's strengths and personality type fit his call.

The same was true of David. What got David noticed and brought him into national leadership roles were his innate strengths—his musical aptitude, his athletic ability (note his skill with a sling), his handsome appearance. As a songwriter, David was good with words. He also exhibited great natural charisma and relational instincts, which immediately attracted people. Saul loved him greatly, but soon regretted it—David's favor with the people rapidly surpassed that of the king himself.

While Calling, Passion, Preparation, and Allegiance were all part of his ascent to the throne, David's innate Design—his strengths, talents, gifts and personality type— was what initially launched his career. Because God created him for his life mission, David's Design provided clues to what he was called to do and be. Similarly, exploring your gifts, strengths, and personality type can yield important clues to your destiny.

What is Design?

Design consists of two complimentary areas: *Strengths* and *Personality Type*. Design is the sum of the innate qualities you were born with: your *nature* (as opposed to *nurture*, which falls under the heading of Preparation). *Strengths* are the talents and aptitudes that make you naturally good at certain things. They let you perform at an exceptional level in a certain area, applying less effort and for greater results.

Personality Types are shorthand language for describing your unique, inner traits. While strengths describe abilities and outward performance, Personality Types attempt to explain your soul's inner workings and how they influence your actions. Type provides a model for understanding how different people think, take in information, make decisions, and relate to both their inner world and the world around them. Types describe what goes on inside your head. (Men, take note: learning personality types might actually help you understand what the women in your life are thinking!) Therefore, your type says a lot about where you excel, what you enjoy, and what roles and activities energize or drain you.

Strengths and Personality Type

Strengths and personality type have much in common, because inward mechanisms and outward performance are connected. I find it helpful to think of the two as an overlapping continuum (see diagram). At the far left end of strengths are purely physical qualities that aren't part of your personality at all, like hand-eye coordination. The right end of the spectrum features things like core motivations or a desire for privacy that aren't strengths or weaknesses, but simply portray your type's individuality.

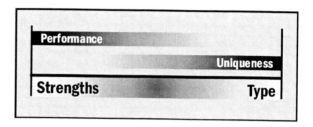

We might say that personality types describe our inner workings, while strengths describe aptitudes for doing certain things. For instance, a "C" on the DiSC™ is inwardly motivated to do things right and bring them to completion (their type), which tends to give them an aptitude for jobs like accounting that require precision with numbers (a strength).

Both personality types and strength systems create sorting categories that offer language to understand human differences. The differences are real; the categories are simply artificial constructs that help us remember and understand the insights.

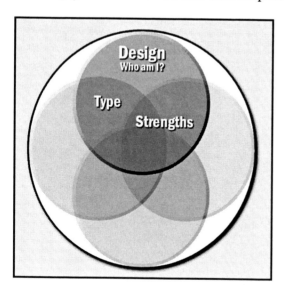

So whether something is a strength or a type quality is much less important than knowing it is there!

Exploring Strengths

Strengths are an important component of life purpose. They can be physical qualities like endurance or quick reflexes that make you good at sports, a pleasing singing voice or the fine motor skills of a surgeon. Strengths can also be aptitudes like an ear for music, a knack for foreign languages or the ability to visualize things in 3-D. These natural talents are what enable you to perform well right out of the gate, ramp up proficiency at an accelerated rate, and consistently operate at an exceptional level. The root of the word strength has to do with power—and strengths are your innate power to do something well.

My children's strengths were visible when they were only a few years old. Taylor is naturally athletic and loves to push the limits of his body. He's the one who had to crawl on *top* of the swing set instead of staying on the seats, who broke his arm trying to climb a tree with no hands. He was first to venture up into the playscapes at McDonald's restaurants, and he loved it. Even though our daughter was two years older, she wouldn't risk the tunnels until he went first.

On the other hand, our daughter was as fearless with people as our son was with heights. At 18 months, she would walk up to people she had never met, crawl into their laps, hand them a book, and expect them to read to her. Her natural aptitude for words and communication has made her into a poet and songwriter as a teen.

Strengths, Skills and Roles

Sometimes we confuse strengths and skills. A skill is *the practiced ability to do a task well.* It's proficiency. However, it is possible to be proficient in something that doesn't come naturally! Have you ever been in a job you could do well but didn't enjoy; or been given a task you could succeed at but that sucked you dry with the extraordinary effort it took to do it well? Skills are not always strengths.

Weaknesses that you've been able to overcome or compensate for are also not strengths. We'll use the term "learned skills" for things you *aren't* innately good at but have become proficient at. If you are naturally weak in an area, you may gain proficiency in it, but the level of effortless excellence displayed by those who are truly gifted in that area will forever remain out of reach. It's only when skills are built on top of natural strengths that truly exceptional long-term performance is possible.

> ### Strengths Are...
>
> 1. Natural, innate abilities. You were born with them and even used them as a kid.
> 2. Areas where you perform at an exceptional level without strain.
> 3. Things you have a knack for learning or pick up quickly.
> 4. Energizing and satisfying to function in.
> 5. Recognized by others when they are used.

And that's the importance of strengths in life purpose discovery. To maximize your impact (especially in the latter stages of Calling development), you must be in a role that allows you to operate out of your strengths, because those are the areas where you can really excel.

A common assumption is that our greatest growth comes from identifying and correcting our weaknesses. For instance, job reviews often focus on pinpointing weaknesses as areas for growth, and tie one's career and compensation to overcoming them. But the authors of the influential book *Now, Discover Your Strengths* turn this conventional wisdom about strengths on its head. The extensive survey the book was based on found that *the greatest performance and growth potential comes from capitalizing on our strengths.* In other words, don't spend your energy trying to improve your natural weaknesses! Instead, find your inborn talents, invest most of your energy into making them world-class strengths, and reshape your roles around them.

Unfortunately, the vast majority of people work in roles that don't allow them to regularly use their best strengths. It's been widely reported that only one in five workers at large companies worldwide use their strengths on a daily basis.

By increasing your conscious awareness of your strengths, you'll be able to choose roles that fit them—which will automatically increase your satisfaction and effectiveness in the workplace.

Limits on Functioning in Strengths

We'd all love to function in our strengths all the time. These factors place limits on our ability to do so:

1. **Failing to build skills on strengths**
   Your abilities are less valuable, and you'll tend to remain in low influence or entry-level roles

2. **Lack of credentials**
   Lack of education, experience, or sponsorship can limit opportunities

3. **Lack of character**
   Blind spots or past failings (like debt or divorce) can limit or eliminate choices

4. **Inability to exercise choice**
   Cultural, economic or political factors (like living under a totalitarian regime) can limit your options

5. **Life stage**
   It is far more likely that you'll be in a best-fit role in your 50's or 60's than in your 20's or 30's.

Character Weaknesses

There are two important caveats to the idea of focusing on strengths. One is that projects and organizations require a balance of strengths to succeed—meaning that if you are going focus on your strengths, you must team with others who have strengths in complementary areas.

The second involves the definition of strengths and weaknesses. In this chapter, a weakness means simply the lack of a certain inborn talent. For instance, leaders who are strong at visioning are often weak at the skills that make for effective implementation. There is nothing wrong with that—focus on developing your visioning abilities and partner with people who are good implementers! But your talents also make you vulnerable to corresponding *character* issues—and that's a whole different ball game. While Saul was a visionary man of action, the flip-side of his strength was the fear of losing control. Saul's inability to deal with his character weakness grew into a debilitating paranoia that greatly undermined his ability to function as a national leader.

The lesson is this. When we are using the word "strength" or "weakness" to refer to inborn *talents*, the best results come from maximizing our top abilities instead of remediating our weaknesses. However, when we are talking about strengths or weaknesses of *character*, the opposite is true. Serious character flaws can destroy a lifetime of work with our best strengths in a single moment. They cannot be ignored. So with talents and abilities, we should focus most of our effort on maximizing our best. With character, focus on dealing with weaknesses.

Identifying Strengths

One potent method for identifying strengths is to do a formal assessment (like Strengths-Finder™). Or, the process can be done informally, by reflecting on your experiences and drawing a list of strengths from them. The exercises for the informal process come directly from the characteristics of strengths (see pg. 41):

1. **Natural, innate abilities**
   Self-inventory: What do you think you are naturally good at? (5.1)

2. **Areas where you perform at an exceptional level without strain**
   Look at successes and identify strengths behind them. (5.3)

3. **Energizing and satisfying to function in**
   Track what is energizing and satisfying and what isn't in your current roles. (5.6)

4. **Recognized by others when used**
   What do those who know you well say are your strengths? (5.4)

> **Strengths-Finder™**
>
> The Strengths-Finder™ system is a powerful way to measure strengths and help you refocus around your best. This assessment defines a strength as "consistent near-perfect performance in an activity." That's a broader definition than what we're using here: to attain near perfect performance means practice and skill development (what we're including under the heading of Preparation) built on top of innate talents. In fact, Strengths-Finder™ is in many ways a business-oriented personality typing system. By separating type and strengths here, we're allowing you to ask, "What is my natural style?" and "What am I good at?" as two separate questions.

Start with the *Strengths Inventory* (5.1). If you get stuck, the *Strengths Examples* worksheet (5.2) and *Strengths Behind Successes* exercise (5.3) will give you additional ideas. If you have created a list but are a little unsure of whether these are legitimate strengths, use the *Strengths Validation* exercise (5.4) to get some feedback from friends or family members on your strengths.

The other exercise you'll want to do up front is the *Identifying Weaknesses* inventory (5.5). Knowing your weaknesses shows you what roles and tasks to avoid!

This self-evaluation helps you get down on paper what you intuitively know about your strengths. Do this exercise *quickly*, and try not to be especially neat or over-analyze what you write: we'll evaluate your jottings later.

Step 1: Brain Dump

List your strengths. What are your natural talents and abilities? What activities come easily to you? What talents in you do people consistently affirm? They can be an athletic abilities, an aptitude for a certain kind of task, or something experience has shown you are really good at. Just jot down whatever comes to mind. When you reach the point where you can't think of any more, flip to the *Strengths Examples* (5.2) and scan for ideas.

Step 2: Cull it Down

Now, step back and look over what you wrote. Eliminate anything that is a learned skill: something that you aren't naturally good at but can do if you have to. Feel free to combine similar items or cross out anything that on second though you don't feel is a strength—just give yourself the benefit of the doubt and leave it on the list if you aren't sure.

Step 3: Top Five

Put a star next to the ones you think are your top five best strengths.

Strengths Examples

Below is a list of generic descriptions of possible strengths. Make them your own! The best statements about your strengths highlight what is truly unique about you.

- ☐ Math/numbers
- ☐ Communication
- ☐ Making friends/networking
- ☐ Introspection
- ☐ Athletics
- ☐ Hand-eye coordination
- ☐ Physical strength/endurance
- ☐ Repetitive tasks
- ☐ Creativity
- ☐ Problem solving
- ☐ Multi-tasking
- ☐ Focusing on one big project
- ☐ Craftsmanship
- ☐ Writing
- ☐ Quick and dirty solutions
- ☐ Learning languages
- ☐ Identifying with people
- ☐ Listening
- ☐ Acting/playing a role
- ☐ Team player
- ☐ Eye for beauty
- ☐ Artistic
- ☐ Sense of direction
- ☐ Visualization
- ☐ Dreaming/brainstorming
- ☐ Getting others on board
- ☐ Facing conflict
- ☐ Good with tools
- ☐ Affirming

- ☐ Risk taking
- ☐ Reasoning
- ☐ Emotional sensitivity
- ☐ Intensity
- ☐ Letting go
- ☐ Living in the moment
- ☐ Music
- ☐ Inspiration
- ☐ Fixing things
- ☐ Building things
- ☐ Designing
- ☐ Managing people or projects
- ☐ Details
- ☐ Storytelling
- ☐ Making people laugh
- ☐ Giving
- ☐ Organizing
- ☐ Delegating
- ☐ Critical thinking
- ☐ Fairness
- ☐ Showing mercy
- ☐ Sticking with it
- ☐ Reflecting
- ☐ Planning
- ☐ Improvising
- ☐ Enthusiasm
- ☐ Decisiveness
- ☐ Seeing the future
- ☐ Having fun

Our strengths are what give us the capacity for top performance, so usually we can find strengths behind our successes. In this exercise, we'll list some successes and try to uncover the strengths that made them possible.

Step 1: List Successes

List at least five significant accomplishments. What have you done that you're proud of? What have others hailed or appreciated about your successes? Where have you won competitions or awards, reached an important goal or made a real difference? Focus on a specific task, project, or event (not a role that stretched over months or years). If you can, pick things in different areas (work, family, sports, service, leadership) and different life stages.

1. _____

2. _____

3. _____

4. _____

5. _____

Step 2: Identify Strengths Behind the Successes

Now take each of your successes or accomplishments in turn. Which of your talents and abilities does this story highlight? What did you bring to the table that made this a success? Which parts came naturally to you or had a big impact with what felt like little effort?

_____

_____

_____

_____

_____

_____

_____

Strengths Validation

Getting feedback is a great way to flesh out your strengths list or gain confidence in what you've already identified. Find a person you know well, with whom you have a strong relationship (your spouse, a family member, or a close colleague), and who is willing to spend 20 minutes helping you. Explain that you'd like honest, objective feedback on your strengths. Then take the following steps:

Step 1: Ask

"What would you say are five natural talents or abilities that I have; that are my best strengths? Where have you seen those abilities in action?" (If your friend is drawing a blank, show him/her the *Strengths Examples* worksheet (5.2)).

1. _____

2. _____

3. _____

4. _____

5. _____

Step 2: Review Your List

Show your friend the strengths and weaknesses that you identified in exercises 5.1 and 5.5, and ask for comments. Add any new insights that seem accurate to your list.

_____

_____

_____

_____

_____

_____

_____

_____

Knowing what you *aren't* good at is an important part of knowing your strengths. Remember, we all have weaknesses. If nobody else was weak where you are strong, you wouldn't have a life purpose!

Step 1: Examine Experiences

Think of several roles or situations where you felt you didn't do well. (Often frustration, stress, ineffectiveness or a lack of confidence are signs of functioning outside our strengths.) In each situation, what were you doing that *wasn't* a strength, didn't come naturally or sapped your energy?

Step 2: Self-Inventory

Now, step back and start to draw from what you already know about yourself. What could you add to your list of things that de-energize you or don't come easily? Where in life do you expend a great deal of energy to get merely adequate results? Add these items to your list. When you can't think of any more, flip to the *Strengths Examples* (5.2) and scan for ideas.

Strengths, Type and Energy  5.6

This workplace exercise helps you identify strengths and explores the fit between your roles and your strengths and personality type.

Step 1: Keep an Energy List (Daily)

Start two lists side-by-side on your laptop, PDA or by placing this *Workbook* page in a place where you will see it throughout the day. One list is what energizes you, while the other is for energy drains. As you work, stop periodically for a few seconds and jot down what you've been doing that energizes or drains you. Keep adding to your list for at least a week.

Step 2: Evaluate (10 minutes)

Since functioning in your strengths tends to be energizing and satisfying, while functioning outside of them is draining, your two lists should tell you something about where your strengths lie. Take 10 minutes to ponder the things that are energizing. What innate strengths are you using in those tasks? Jot down those strengths below. Then go through the same process with the things that drain you. What does that tell you about where your weaknesses are?

Energizing Strengths	Draining Weaknesses

Chapter 6: Design/ Personality Type

"It makes you wonder. All the brilliant things we might have done with our lives if only we suspected we knew how."

General Benjamin in *Bel Canto*

Personality type is a specialized language created to describe human differences. Personality systems categorize us in areas like thinking patterns, decision-making style, what kinds of information we tune into, how we exert influence, etc. These differences are grouped into "types," usually organized by theories about what makes up human personality.

Understanding type makes a huge difference in building great relationships, finding your destiny role and dealing with people. For instance, if I am talking to a leader who is a "D" on the DiSC™ profile, I am working with a hard-charging, task-oriented individual who likes to cut to the chase and take action. With a high "D," I move the conversation along quickly, speak in a very direct manner and appeal to the person's competitive nature to get top performance.

Or if I'm helping a "P" on the Myers-Briggs© to improve focus and time management, I know I'm working with someone who has a play ethic. If you're a "P," you either play first and then work, or you make work into play (as opposed to "J's," who only play when the work is done). "P's" like to continue gathering information and keep their options open as long as possible, which can make it a struggle for them to adapt to the deadline driven "J" working world. Most time-management tools were developed by "J's" (the opposite of the "P" type) who love clarity and closure, and they can drive "P's" nuts.

One of my "P" coaching clients had an especially tough time with this. He'd vacillate between trying to time-block everything and work from a to-do list, to feeling so tied down by the structure that he'd let his life and his calendar spiral out of control. Talking about managing his time according to the natural tendencies of his type was a revelation. He discovered that what worked best for him was a varied schedule, not rigid time blocking. As long as he had adequate opportunities to choose in the moment what to work on, he could schedule things and get them done without feeling boxed in.

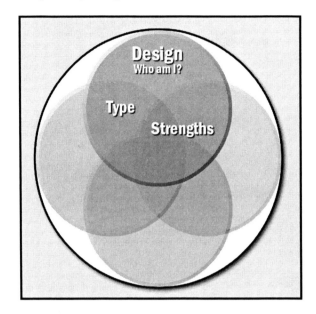

Aligning with your type's natural working style tends to raise the energy level, improve performance, and often leads to insights like "I'm not the lazy, can't-meet-a-deadline time-management failure I always thought I was!"

There is so much you can do with type. You can:

- Become more self-aware.
- Understand why some roles work for you and some don't.
- Make better decisions about what commitments to take on.
- Gain a whole lot of new understanding of your spouse and children.
- Figure out the natural language of the people around you to improve communication.
- Disarm conflicts by explaining the type dynamics that caused them.
- Create roles for people on your team that fit who they are and cause them to flourish.

Understanding Type

There are five levels of type understanding you can attain (see box on the next page). Most people come into the discovery process at level I or level II. The payoff with type begins at level III: grasping it well enough to understand your own Design. For instance, if you are a "C" on the DiSC™, the assessment will help you understand your drive to do things with excellence, and give you a wealth of helpful tips on how to channel that drive in productive ways.

However, the biggest benefits come when you go beyond learning your own style and focus on others. For the leader, reaching level IV or V gives you an in-depth grasp of others' types—and that is truly powerful! For example, if you are a "D" working with a "C," you'll know your quick-and-dirty approach to cutting through the red tape and getting things done no matter what can conflict with the "C's" desire to comply with the rules and make sure the job is done well. If you are going to work together, that's an area you'll need to address.

<table>
<tr><td colspan="2">

Type: Levels of Understanding

Level I: Don't know my type.

Level II: Know the letters but don't know what they mean.

Level III: Know my own type and understand what it means.

Level IV: Know my type and that of those around me, and use that understanding to communicate and relate more effectively.

Level V: Type expert. Can help others identify and understand their type and how it interacts with others' types.

</td></tr>
</table>

But an even better approach is to strategically make use of that difference to help both of you succeed. As a "D," you dislike details and are probably better at starting than finishing. Your "C" co-worker, on the other hand, loves details and is a great finisher. So if you can negotiate how to divide up your projects, together you can accomplish much more to a much higher standard than you ever could alone. One of the best investments you can make in your career, your ministry abilities and your family and friendships is to choose a type system and really master it.

Type Assessment

The process of understanding your type starts with a formal assessment. We've created a special deal for you to get a on-line DiSC™ profile at www.ALeadersLifePurpose.com at a steep discount. The assessment takes only 15 to 20 minutes. Once you've finished, a personalized, 25-page report will be e-mailed to you explaining your unique type. You'll get valuable information on things like what motivates you, how you respond to conflict, the management style that suits you best, how to relate to other types and much more.

While personality assessments are rigorously tested to ensure they give accurate results, you still need to validate your profile. Sit down with a coach and go through your report to make sure this description really fits—or if there is a slightly different type that's a better fit. A stopgap measure if you don't have a chance to do this with a professional is the *Peer Validation* exercise

An on-line DiSC™ Assessment at a special discounted group rate is available through www.ALeadersLifePurpose.com

(6.1). Another great way to build on your report is to find a book that describes the various types, so you can learn about the whole typing system and not just your own profile. Books like *The Personality Code* by Bradberry or the *4-Dimensional Manager* by Straw will help you with DiSC™. For Myers-Briggs© try *Type-Talk* or *Type-Talk at Work* by Kroeger. For even more feedback (and a good time in the bargain) try the *Type Night* exercise (6.2) with your family, friends or your team at work.

Peer Validation

The people who know you well almost surely have valuable insights to offer about how you operate in your type. This exercise helps confirm what your type is and offers insight on how others see you.

Sit down for half an hour with a close friend, family member or spouse—someone who has known you for many years—and discuss your personality profile. Have your friend read through your profile (from a book or report) with you. Use these questions to guide your discussion:

- Have your friend point out the four or five characteristics that best fit you in this profile.
- Ask what insights this profile provides about who you are and how to relate to you.
- Can your friend think of a story or two that illustrates some of these type characteristics?
- How do these qualities influence the way you lead and do your job?
- What does this profile explain about you that most people don't understand?

This is a great game to play at extended family gatherings and reunions, with your immediate family (when your kids are old enough), or with a team at work. It will help you understand each other better, and provide a lot of good laughs along the way!

You'll need a book on a personality system you are somewhat familiar with that includes several-page profiles of each type (Try *Type Talk* by Kroeger for MBTI©, *Discover Your God-Given Gifts* by Fortune for motivational gifts, or *The Personality Code* by Bradberry for DiSC™). Your group will need to be comfortable and secure with each other. This game may not work well in dysfunctional families or teams!

Step 1: Agree on Ground Rules

Create a set of ground rules like those below that everyone can agree on:

1. Focus on positive qualities, instead of negative ones. Make this a time that draws you closer and builds everyone up.
2. Honor each other. Don't tell stories that embarrass or hurt people.
3. Be honest if the discussion gets into a sensitive area of your life you'd rather not have others talk about.
4. If you feel like the description of another type fits you better, you can switch at any time.

Step 2: Figure out Your Types

If the book includes an assessment, have everybody take it. Some type books have word-choice lists that everyone can look at to make a tentative determination of their type.

Step 3: Validate

Have each person read their type profile out loud. After each sentence or two, have the reader say whether they think that characteristic fits them or not. If you aren't sure or want feedback, ask the rest of the group for input. The idea is to validate whether this is actually your type. If the description isn't a great fit, try looking at some other types that are slightly different and see if they fit better. Make sure you go first on this step and take the risk of being vulnerable first!

Step 4: Tell Stories (Optional)

Once everyone has validated their type, see if you can think of some family history stories or humorous examples of how different members functioned in their types or interacted with each other. Remember to follow the ground rules, stay positive and build each other up!

My Ideal Team

Teams can benefit greatly from understanding type, because it allows them to adjust roles to fit each person's natural style. This exercise helps team leaders identify their strengths, then lists the strengths and types needed as complements.

You can also use this exercise to form teams or create convergent roles. If you aren't certain what types would best compliment you, ask your coach for help.

1. What does this team need to be able to do with excellence? What strengths or type characteristics do those tasks require? List them on the left.

2. Which of these qualities does your type provide? Underline them.

3. Identify any learned skills in your role—things you can do but don't come naturally. What types would love to do that kind of thing and could take it off your plate?

4. Which abilities do you lack? What types would provide them? (For ideas, you may want to leaf through the profiles of different types, and ask yourself what unique abilities of each type are most needed on this team.)

5. What are the weak areas for my type? Which types could complement those weaknesses?

Quality or Strength Needed on Team	Types or People that Offer It

Question 3: Why Do I Desire *This?* (Passion)

"The giants of the faith all had one thing in common: neither victory nor success, but passion."

Phillip Yancey

Passion is the underlying motivation and energy behind our life purpose. Our Passions define what's most important to us, what we really care about and what we energetically pursue. They're the urges that compel us to *do* something.

Passion for justice is what led William Wilberforce to get slavery outlawed in England. A passionate desire to show mercy kept Mother Teresa working a lifetime in the slums of Calcutta. Without the dynamism of Passion, we never engage our life mission with the drive and enthusiasm necessary to pull it off.

Here are some keys to understanding the place of Passion in life purpose:

- **Passions motivate and energize us**
  They provide the drive to overcome obstacles and persevere in the pursuit of dreams.

- **Passions align with values**
  We are most passionate about what we hold to most deeply.

- **Dreams are a window to the heart**

Even dreams that seem frivolous or impossible draw back the curtain on our Passions, our deepest desires and our values.

- **Obstacles block Passion**
  When we do dream, we often tend to see the immediate obstacles and get stuck. If instead of stopping we allow our Passion to energize us, we (or God) might find a way.

- **We can test dreams by their motivations**
  Looking at *why* we want to pursue a dream and what drives it helps us make a sound decision on whether or not to pursue it.

As the motivation behind our most important pursuits, Passion is an essential part of life purpose. The three main areas of Passion we'll mine for these life purpose clues are *Energy*, *Dreams* and *Values*.

The Energy of Passion

Paul discussed his Passion— preaching the gospel to the entire known world—as something that drove him, that energized him , even as a "compulsion" (I Cor. 9:16). "For this I toil, striving with all the **energy** which he mightily inspires in me" (Col. 1:29; RSV). That passionate energy took him across the known world, ignited by the desire to preach the gospel to the far reaches of the Roman Empire.

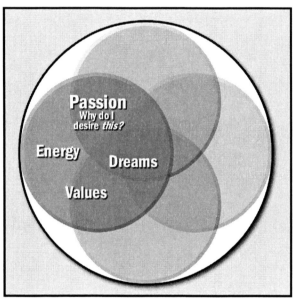

What most energizes you? One way to find out is simply becoming more aware of how you express your Passion. When we speak, our voice tone, volume and emotive content vary over time. For example, read the following two sentences aloud:

- "I'm not sure what is causing us to misunderstand each other."
- "I am *so frustrated* with her! Every time we talk it feels like we are hurling grenades at each other."

The energy in these two sentences is very different. The first is cool and analytic, while the second is animated and emotive. The person in the second sentence is talking about something he is passionate about. It's the same way with all dreams and desires—when you get on a subject that is really meaningful to you, you'll speak with more emotion. Your voice tone and volume may change. You may speak more rapidly, in a gush of words. The way you talk about your life reveals where your Passions are.

The general rule is, follow the energy to identify the Passion—the values, dreams and desires that you care most deeply about.

One way to follow the energy to Passions is a technique I call *Listening for Significance*. This works great for getting to the bottom of a dream or value. It's very simple: you watch a friend or your spouse for these energy cues, pick out the word or phrase that seemed to have the most energy behind it, and ask the person to expand on it. For instance, with the example above, the question might be:

- *"You mentioned your conversation 'felt like we are hurling grenades.' Say more about that."*
- *"Tell me more about what makes you so frustrated."*

Notice the underlined words—those phrases are directly quoted from the person you are listening to. This technique is very simple but powerful if you stick with it: repeat a significant phrase, and use a very simple query: "Tell me more about that." This simple question is intentionally vague—it allows the person to answer any way they want to, instead of you directing the conversation.

You can also use reflection exercises to look at your life and find places of Passion. Since heightened energy often points to Passion, these action steps involve looking at various activities and seeing which ones energize or drain you, as in the *Energy Activities* exercise (7.2). The *Passion Bull's Eye* (7.1) aims to identify Passions from your self-knowledge, without first looking at energizing activities. If you struggle with this, go back to the *Energy Activities* exercise (7.2) and keep a list during the week to give you some additional information to build on.

The Passion Bull's Eye

This exercise explores the causes, ideals, and themes that you are passionate about. Use the questions below to identify them, then place each one on the Bull's Eye with the strongest Passions toward the center. We're looking for ideals here, so if you think of an activity you love (like windsurfing), try to name the underlying passion (fitness, being outdoors). Think of passions within each of the *Life Wheel Categories* (8.2) to get a balanced view.

- What *causes* have I invested in long term? Where have I volunteered or contributed over the years, because I cared deeply about the cause?

- What are my *soapbox issues?* These are the issues and ideas I talk about all the time, argue over with people, get animated or upset about.

- What *needs* tug at my heart? What's the need I can't keep myself from meeting?

- What in my life brings my *emotions* to the surface? What do I see or think of that gets me choked up or compels me to take action?

- What am I most excited and joyful about in life? Most grieved over?

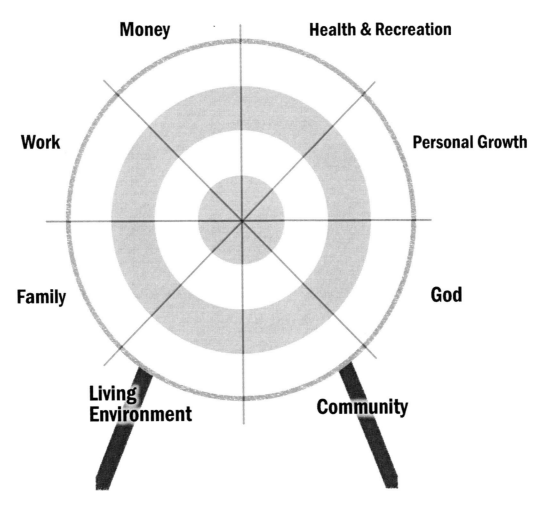

This reflection (similar to *Strengths, Type and Energy,* 5.6) gives you another way to identify what gives you energy, and therefore may connect to your passions. We'll create a list of what engages and energizes you in life, and then mine it for insights.

Step 1: Roles and Responsibilities

Start by thinking about the different roles you fill in life: employee, student, spouse, friend, parent, or volunteer. What activities really stoke you? What do you think about or anticipate even when you aren't doing it? If it's hard to think of examples, pull out last month's calendar and look it over. Don't over-analyze—just try to get some examples down on paper.

Step 2: Fun and Fellowship

Add to your list from other areas of life: hobbies, church involvement, recreation, interests. We're not looking for what's productive, but what you are drawn to. What things in life do you give your best energy to and get the most energy back from?

Step 3: Find the Themes

Now examine your list for clues to your core passions using these questions:

- *Why* do you care about these things? What is behind them that energizes you?
- What stands out or surprises you as you look at this list?
- What themes appear repeatedly on this list? (i.e. "working with kids.")
- If you had to sum up what energizes you in all these different things in only three or four phrases, what would they be?

Chapter 8: Passion/Dreams and Desires

"I am not unmindful that some of you have come here out of great trials and tribulations. Some of you have come fresh from narrow cells. Some of you have come from areas where your quest for freedom left you battered by the storms of persecution and staggered by the winds of police brutality. You have been the veterans of creative suffering. Continue to work with the faith that unearned suffering is redemptive. Go back to Mississippi, go back to Alabama, go back to South Carolina, go back to Georgia, go back to Louisiana, go back to the slums and ghettos of our northern cities, knowing that somehow this situation can and will be changed.

Let us not wallow in the valley of despair. I say to you today, my friends, that in spite of the difficulties and frustrations of the moment, I still have a dream. It is a dream deeply rooted in the American dream.

I have a dream that one day this nation will rise up and live out the true meaning of its creed: 'We hold these truths to be self-evident: that all men are created equal.'

I have a dream that one day on the red hills of Georgia the sons of former slaves and the sons of former slave owners will be able to sit down together at a table of brotherhood.

I have a dream that one day even the state of Mississippi, a desert state, sweltering with the heat of injustice and oppression, will be transformed into an oasis of freedom and justice.

I have a dream that my four children will one day live in a nation where they will not be judged by the color of their skin but by the content of their character.

*I have a **dream** today!*

I have a dream that one day the state of Alabama, whose governor's lips are presently dripping with the words of interposition and nullification, will be transformed into a situation where little black boys and black girls will be able to join hands with little white boys and white girls and walk together as sisters and brothers.

*I have a **dream** today!*

I have a dream that one day every valley shall be exalted, every hill and mountain shall be made low, the rough places will be made plain, and the crooked places will be made straight, and the glory of the Lord shall be revealed, and all flesh shall see it together.

This is our hope. This is the faith with which I return to the South. With this faith we will be able to hew out of the mountain of despair a stone of hope. With this faith we will be able to transform the jangling discords of our nation into a beautiful symphony of brotherhood. With this faith we will be able to work together, to pray together, to struggle together, to go to jail together, to stand up for freedom together, knowing that we will be free one day."

Dr. Martin Luther King Jr., 1963

Dreams are powerful. Dreams and those who dream them can change cultures, redirect nations and move mountains. Dreams animate our hearts with passionate energy, spur us to action, and offer the hope that a better future is not only possible but imperative. Dreams are the images of our Passion overlaid on the future.

In the context of life purpose, dreams can be defined as *"pictures of the future we hope to live in someday."* They are snapshots of what we desire life to look like. By contrast, a goal is an end that we have committed to accomplishing. Dreams simply look at the future and say, "This is what I wish for."

A dream becomes a goal when you commit to reaching in within a certain time frame. But part of the power of dreams is that you *don't* have to have practical plans to reach them. You don't have to be committed to making a dream happen—it is simply a picture of what the future might look like if it is in accord with your desires. The fact that we don't have to have a realistic plan frees us to imagine what we really want without being bound by what we feel is possible.

"Vision" is another term that gets confused with dreams. A vision is a dream-goal that reaches out to capture others to work for its fulfillment. It is a visual picture of a desired future that a visionary has committed to make happen by bringing others on board to help. If your visions are simply ideas for a neat future that

> *The currency of dreams is hope; visions run instead on faith.*

you hope might happen someday, you are a dreamer, not a visionary. The currency of dreams is *hope*; visions run instead on *faith*, the substance of things hoped for.

Dream Principles

Martin Luther King's "I Have a Dream" speech illustrates a number of important dreaming principles we can apply to life purpose discovery:

1. **Dreams are visual images**
   Notice the abundant imagery in King's speech. He carries you to "the red hills of Georgia," to a future where "little black boys and girls will be able to join hands with little white boys and girls and walk together as brothers." Visual images affect us much more deeply and are more powerfully motivating than words. That's what makes *Envisioning Your Dream* (exercise 8.4) so powerful.

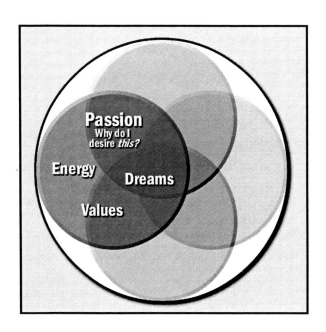

2. **Dreams reveal deep desires**
   King's dream touches us at a visceral, emotional level because it expresses the heart-cry of an entire people for freedom and justice. Dreams are like that: they resonate with the Passions of our hearts. We'll use *Dream Themes* (8.5) to find the deep desires that lie beneath your dreams.

3. **Dreams motivate**
   Martin Luther King spoke about his dream of a better future to motivate African Americans to keep working for equality and keep hoping for non-violent change. Dreams motivate because visualizing them activates the hope that they can be reached. This chapter includes two techniques for increasing motivation: *Envisioning* the dream fulfilled (8.4) and looking at the cost of not reaching a dream (exercise 9.2).

4. **Dreams ignore obstacles**
   Notice how King urges his audience to *"Go back... knowing that somehow this situation can and will be changed."* The dream is that inequality will be changed somehow; that we don't know how it will happen it is immaterial to the fact that this is a dream worth pursuing.

6. **Dreams connect us to heaven**
   Because they describe an ideal world, dreams have a certain otherworldly

quality. King states, "...we will not be satisfied until 'justice rolls down like waters, and righteousness like a mighty stream.'" King's dream is in fact a picture of heaven—and in that sense, every true dream is grounded in heaven, because every true desire was created to find its ultimate fulfillment there.

Dreams and Purpose

The specific future you dream about says a lot about your life purpose. If you dream of opening a Bed and Breakfast inn and having the chance to host all kinds of people, that dream may be a container for your deepest desires in life. So let's take a look at what you dream.

A great place to start is with a *Dream Inventory* (8.1). This version is broken into two sections: one for Big Dreams, and a second for Fun Dreams. Big dreams are desires depicted in larger pieces: getting a master's degree, starting a business, mentoring five young leaders or going to the mission field. Many fall under the second level of God's purposes—working to bring His Kingdom to life in the world (see diagram). Fun dreams aren't so much about legacy as about joy. They fall under the third level of purpose. Maybe you've always wanted to hike down the Oregon coast with three friends, take a hot air balloon ride or visit the grandchildren regularly. Consult the *Life Wheel Categories* (8.2) while you do this exercise to make sure you dream in all areas of life, and not just about ministry or your career.

Creating a *Dream Lifestyle* (8.3) is another way to uncover fun dreams. Describing the living situation, workplace, home, schedule and relationships that you'd really love can make it easier to voice what would bring joy in life.

> ### Dreams and Limitations
>
> It is important that we keep in mind that dreams are remembrances of Eden. We can imagine an ideal life where all things turn out well, but we cannot fully reproduce it in this broken world. A dream is an echo of the eternal, running down through time to a fallen race. Although we may pursue them here, our deepest desires only find ultimate fulfillment in heaven.
>
> Does that mean we should stop dreaming or pursuing dreams? Absolutely not! We must dream, to keep heaven in mind and to understand how this world falls far short of it. Without dreams, we easily settle into pragmatic worldliness.

It's worthwhile just to inventory your dreams. But using them as life purpose clues requires finding the Passions that underlie your dreams. Why do you want to pursue this particular dream? What would it give you, and the people you want to serve? Why this, and not something else? From big, hairy audacious goals that change the world to innocent wishes for fun experiences, all dreams are a window into your heart's desire. They are *containers* that give form to your Passions, so you can visualize and talk about them.

The *Dream Themes* exercise (8.5) provides a structure for finding desires under dreams. It can be especially interesting to look for themes in your *Fun Dreams*. People are often amazed at what their smaller dreams can reveal about who they are and

Freedom to Dream

Here are some tips for dreaming freely:

- **Dream in pencil**
  Dreams are containers for your passions. You can always change the container.

- **Create a "Dream Space"**
  Give yourself unlimited resources, or the knowledge that you can't fail.

- **Don't worry about implementation**
  Dreams don't need a plan—they are a picture of the future you desire.

- **There is no "right" answer**
  You don't get extra points for having things turn out exactly as you envision.

what they value.

If there is a particular dream you want to pursue, the *Envisioning Your Dream* exercise (8.4) helps you flesh it out in detail. This is a visualization exercise, so make sure you picture the specifics of the dream instead of just putting down generalities like, "this would help people." Who specifically would you help, and how? The more detail the better.

Keep in mind that different personalities have different dreaming styles. The most striking difference is between "S's" and "N's" on the Myers-Briggs©. "N's" are natural dreamers: they are future-oriented, conceptual thinkers who easily create dream pictures that are disconnected from the present (in other words, they can dream without needing a plan to get there.) "S's," on the other hand, are practical and present oriented. They dream by extrapolating concrete past or present experiences into the future. Dreaming without a connection to present reality is frustrating and meaningless for them.

Dream exercises come more naturally to "N's", but "S's" can enjoy them if they start with times in the past where they've experienced what they love, and extrapolate those real events into a picture of their desired future. If you are one of these concrete thinkers, use your natural dreaming style, and don't feel like you have to create the future out of nothing!

Testing Dreams

I'd like to go to Bora Bora in the South Seas some day, and stay in one of those bamboo cabanas that are built out over a blue-green tropical lagoon. I'd sit with my feet dangling in the clear, warm water, watch the sun go down, see the moon rise over the surf and rock to sleep on the waves.

Sounds wonderful, doesn't it? There is nothing wrong with dreaming about it—in

God's Purposes

fact, that kind of dream gets me thinking about heaven, if I hold it loosely. But if I cling to it, and make Bora Bora my passionate pursuit and the focus of my life, not only will that trip fail to satisfy me, but it will mess up the rest of my life, too. This goes back to the purpose diagram: a desire for temporal happiness (level III) has grown out of proportion and displaced being with God and bringing in His Kingdom (levels I and II) as the focus of life.

Money and sexuality are similar. They are not intrinsically bad things, but can be pursued in destructive ways. Much of the content of our dreams falls into this innocent, neutral ground, where the object of the dream is neither good nor bad; it is how we go after it that makes the difference. Any temporal pleasure elevated to the status of a primary purpose brings death, not life.

Our Passions fall into three categories:

- **True Desires** which reflect the image of Christ and point us toward heaven.
- **Innocent Desires** that are part of being human and are neutral.
- **Corrupt Desires** where true or innocent desires are twisted into sinful, destructive forms.

When our desires go awry they tend to be either True Desires pursued in the wrong way, or Innocent Desires taken out of proportion. Sex out of wedlock is often a true desire for intimacy pursued in the wrong way. Arranging your life around getting to Bora Bora is an innocent desire taken way out of proportion. The book of James teaches that desires tend to become corrupted when they are unmet, and they are unmet when the focus is on fulfilling them instead of being with God:

> **Blind Pursuit**
>
> *Blind Pursuit* happens when we reach for something that we know we shouldn't, and we intentionally ignore the warning signs so we can keep running after it. Here are four indicators of Blind Pursuit, with a question for each:
>
> - **Pressure to have it now**
>   *"What is driving the urgency for this? Does it need to happen now, or could you wait?"*
> - **The beneficiary is me**
>   *"Who except you benefits from this dream?"*
> - **Ignoring the impact on those around me**
>   *"How will this affect your spouse? Your kids? How will it impact your friendships?"*
> - **I avoid examining future implications**
>   *"Play out the impact this course of action will have on the next few years of your life."*

"What causes wars, and what causes fightings among you? Is it not your passions that are at war in your members? You desire and do not have, so you kill. And you covet and cannot obtain, so you fight and wage war. You do not have, because you do not ask. And you ask and do not receive, because you ask wrongly, to spend it on your passions." (James 4:1-3; RSV).

Desire itself is not wrong. James (who is about as hard-core as they come) actually says that the right thing to do with a desire is ask God for it! But he offers one caveat: Passion is not meant to help me get mine, but to lead me to serve. So Passions can be tested in terms of *proportion* and *pursuit*: is this dream in proper proportion with other things in life, and is it worthy of making it a primary pursuit?

Begin jotting down as many of your dreams for your future as you can think of. Dreams are what you'd like to do someday. Are there big things you've wanted to accomplish, significant milestones to reach, or a difference you dream of making in the world? Put them under "Big Dreams" below. Fun Dreams are what would bring joy to life. Is there a place you've always wanted to go, an experience you'd love to have, or something cool you want to do just for the sake of doing? Jot these down under "Fun Dreams" on the next page.

To fill out your list, try thinking of dreams in the *Life Wheel Categories* (8.2): *God, Work, Money, Living Environment, Personal Growth, Health and Recreation, Community* and *Family.*

Breaking life down into categories can help you identify a balance of dreams in all areas and minimize the tendency to forget something important. We're going to use the same eight categories from the *Life Wheel Assessment* found in the book *Coaching Questions* as our dreaming, values and Preparation categories. Consult the list below to see what might fit in each area.

Life Wheel Assessment

God
Family
Work
Money
Community
Living Environment
Health & Recreation
Personal Growth

Work
Your job, career or vocation. (For stay-at-home parents, keeping the family running is your vocation!)

Money
Finances, retirement, investments, spending and saving habits, giving, etc.

Living Environment
Your physical surroundings: house, car, yard, bedroom, and the things you own that make up that environment.

Personal Growth
What you do to develop yourself: education, training, learning projects, reading, personal accountability—anything that expands your world, develops new abilities or creates personal change.

Health and Recreation
Hobbies, sports, fitness, diet, health care, sleep, Sabbath, vacations—the things that take care of your mind, body and emotional health.

Community
Relationships with friends and neighbors, plus your community service: PTA, politics, volunteering, boards, service projects, etc.

Family
Your spouse, children and extended family relationships.

God
Your personal relationship with God plus involvement in religious activities: devotions, church involvement, leadership roles, retreat, spiritual disciplines, etc.

What's your dream lifestyle? Picture your surroundings and daily patterns in the future when you are living what you think would be a great life for you. The object is not to pick whatever's most expensive or comfortable—dream about a lifestyle you could actually live, that fits your design and lets you do what you love. Have fun with this: envision where in the world you'd live, your home, your ideal workplace, your schedule, your activities, the people you'd be working with, or your average day. The idea is to get what you really want out on the table in detail so you can see what's there. If you are not a natural dreamer, look to the past and present for ideal situations and put them together to build a picture of your desired future.

Group Option: Collages

Get a bunch of magazines, cut out pictures that represent your ideal life, and paste them to poster board. After an hour or so of cutting and pasting, share your collages with each other. Explain why you chose each picture and what it represents.

Envisioning Your Dream

Take a big dream or vision, and picture what your life will look like when you have accomplished it. Don't worry about *how* you'll get there—just envision what life will look like when you do! Visualize where you'll be living, your surroundings (home or office), the ages of your family members, what kind of people you'd be working with, and any other details you can think of—the more the better. Walk through an average day in a future where you'd reached this dream and record what you see.

This exercise identifies themes in your dreams and the underlying deep desires that animate those dreams.

Step 1: Identify Themes

Look over your *Dream Inventory* (8.1). Do several dreams seem to work toward the same end? Which dreams are connected, and how? (Glance at the *Passion Bull's Eye* exercise (7.1) as well, if you did it.) Find the themes that run through your dreams. If you aren't seeing the connections, sit down with a friend and ask what connections they see in your dream list.

Step 2: Name the Passions

Look over these themes, and name the underlying passions that animate each one. Why do I dream these particular dreams? What does each theme give me? What does this say that I care about?

Theme	Underlying Passion

Chapter 9: Passion/Dream Obstacles

"If at first the idea is not absurd, then there is no hope for it."

Albert Einstein

J ack and his wife were at loggerheads. *"We took a family vacation back to North Carolina last month,"* he declared with exasperation. *"And now every day they keep talking about going back. I don't want to rain on their parade, but I don't see how that's possible."*

"What's behind those feelings?"

"For Joyce, she's always loved the North Carolina weather, the scenery and the culture. She's had a hard time fitting in here, so that's been an issue, too. With the kids, it's probably friends and the familiar versus another new place."

"So if you asked her what she wants, what do you think she'd say?"

"That she wants to go back. She'd say it in a heartbeat."

"And I take it you see things differently?"

"Well, I thought we decided this is where I was called to go. We prayed together and came to agreement, it's a dream position, it is right in line with my career goals—but now she's dug in her heels and there doesn't seem to be any middle ground. I'd be willing to do it for her, but there's no job for me in North Carolina, and who knows what I'd have to take to find one in a month. A 50% pay cut is not going to make her happy, either. And I've

already resigned, so we can't stay here."

"So either way, you have some big obstacles to surmount. I'm curious—if your wife really wanted to live in North Carolina, did that come out when you were deciding on this position?"

"That's what really frustrates me. I felt like this was God's call, and she agreed with it—but now she's off on a different tack."

"So have you talked about this?"

"Tried to," Jack said despondently. "If I start talking about the hard facts, she starts into the 'you care about your job more than me' thing, gets in a passive-aggressive mode and things go downhill from there. I really want to be together in this, but I don't know how to make it happen. This is the third time now we've been through something like this—where she believes in one choice but then can't be happy with it—and I don't want to go through that again."

Obstacles affect all areas of the purpose diagram, but they are most prominent with dreams. In this story, Joyce submerged her dreams in preference to Jack's—until the vacation brought her desires back to the surface at full force, and their prior plans and agreements (plus their finances) stood in the way of her dream. From Jack's point of view, his ideal job seemed within his grasp until agreement with his wife became an obstacle. Neither of the two seemed in touch with the internal obstacles that were making the conflict so intractable.

An obstacle is something that stands in the way of thinking rationally about and pursuing your life purpose. Coaches talk about two major types of obstacles: external and internal. An external obstacle is a circumstance that seems to block progress—like Jack finding a job in North Carolina (for Joyce's dream). External obstacles are any people, circumstances and resources (or lack thereof) that keep you from your dreams ls.

Internal obstacles block us when our thinking patterns throw a wrench in the gears of forward progress. Where external obstacles tend to be fairly easy to identify, internal obstacles are buried deep within our psyche. What keeps Joyce from being able to identify and articulate her true desires to Jack? Maybe she was disappointed so many times growing up that she decided not to hope for things anymore. Or it could be she believes it is not important to God for her to live in a place she loves. These are examples of internal obstacles.

Sometimes internal obstacles can even be dearly held principles or beliefs. One of my own inner obstacles was the belief that "If the relationship is broken, something is wrong with me." That belief kept me from letting go of broken relationships, led me into unhealthy situations and prevented me from standing up for what was right. Even after enduring several extremely painful situations, it took a year with a counselor to bring it to light and realign that area of my heart with Scripture.

Dealing with External Obstacles

External obstacles don't usually lurk in hiding. Most people can tell you exactly what they are: "I don't have time to follow that dream"; or, "I don't have the credentials for that." I call these obstacles "The Big Five":

1. **Money:** There's never enough
2. **Time:** Ditto
3. **Opportunity:** You have the ability but not the chance to show it
4. **Ability:** You lack some particular knowledge or skill needed to pull this off
5. **People:** Either you need them to get on board, or you need them to get out of the way!

Practical tools work well for external solutions. Take a dream you want to pursue, and use the *Identifying Obstacles* exercise (9.1) to see what barriers you'll have to deal with. Then ask a coach or a friend to help you develop at least five creative new options for overcoming each obstacle. The box on the next page provides six categories of solutions you can explore for ideas.

> ### Questions for the Big Five
>
> - *"Give me some options: where could you come up with the money you need to pursue this?"*
> - *"What changes to your schedule, your resources or your timeline could give you the time you need to do this?"*
> - *"Where could the opportunity you need come from? What actions could increase your chances of getting it?"*
> - *"Who do you know that has the answer or could teach you to do this?"*
> - *"Could you accomplish 80% of this dream on 20% of the resources? What might that look like?"*

Another coaching technique for dealing with obstacles is *Regrets* (9.2). Most of us have done at least some thinking about the cost of pursuing our dreams. We make budgets, estimate the time it will take, and wrestle with the sacrifices that dream might require. However, it is much rarer to find a person who has truly examined the cost of **not** following a dream. That's the idea of regrets: you evaluate the cost of *not* moving forward. Exercise 9.2 walks you through this process for a dream or vision.

If you hit on an internal obstacle, you may want to try the *Needs, Losses and Bonds* exercise (4.2) to help you find the underlying reason for what is stymieing you.

Obstacles and Expectations

The bigger your dream, the more you should expect obstacles. If this was easy, someone else would have done it already. We often forget that our life call is about becoming and not just doing. *The process of following your call will make you into the person you are called to be,* just as becoming the person you are called to be will enable you to accomplish your life mission. Obstacles are the training ground of your Calling. They do not prevent you from becoming who you are called to be; on the contrary, they teach you to become that person. You cannot fulfill your destiny without gaining what your obstacles give you.

Frankly, one of the most debilitating obstacles Christians face is their expectations about obstacles. We expect that when God is in something, it will work—that the evidence of being right with God is when things go smoothly and succeed. So when we hit obstacles in life, we are surprised, deflated and disillusioned. We thought the deal was that we'd found the right way in serving God, and in return He'd ensure we experienced favorable circumstances. So when suffering does come, the fear that we've missed it is piled on top of what is already a bad experience.

But I expect you to have trouble in this life, just like Paul. Some of you will be poor so that others might become rich, like Mother Teresa. It wouldn't surprise me if God lets your business crater to gain your heart. Because God's plan encompasses suffering as well as success, these difficulties are what make you into who you were born to be, and empower you to bring others into relationship with God. The promise is that "*in* all these things [sufferings] we are more than conquerors" (Rom. 8:37; RSV). Jesus came to meet us in the midst of this broken world, not to take us out of it. "Many are the afflictions of the righteous, but the Lord delivers him out of them all" (Ps. 34:19).

Dealing with Internal Obstacles

We hit internal obstacles when our inner beliefs, principles or healing issues get in the way of a dream. Usually we can't name our own internal obstacles until we bump up against the blockages they produce. Here are some common symptoms of internal obstacles:

1. Inability to dream or unusual limitations on dreaming.

2. You are stuck—you can't seem to move forward and don't know why.

4. Irrational fears or beliefs that don't fit known facts.

5. Inability to face people or situations.

6. Repeated playback of negative labels (as in, your dad said you'd never amount to anything, and it comes to mind every time you step out into a new venture).

Categories of Solutions

Here are several general categories of solutions for external obstacles:

1. **People.** Who could help? Who would know the answer?

2. **Objectives.** What if you changed the dream or your timeline for it? How could you realize 80% of it with 20% of the resources?

3. **Dream vs. Desire.** What is the desire under this dream? What other ways could you pursue that desire?

4. **Learning.** Where could you find an answer? How could you learn this?

5. **Expectations.** How can I realign my expectations with what is realistically possible?

6. **Self.** What am I doing that is causing this? What could I change about me that would make a difference?

Internal obstacles cause us to do things that don't make sense. For instance, "Why can't I generate any dreams that aren't ministry-related?" or "Why do I feel so unqualified when my resume says I am?" Obviously, other people will have an easier time pointing out our obstacles than we will!

But you have a good reason for what you do. Emotions have a logic all their own. When a belief is damaging or self-sabotaging, it isn't that you said, "I think I'll take on a self-defeating belief today!" Somehow that belief is useful or makes sense to you. It's when you identify the *reason* for the belief that you'll have the most success in changing it. The *Needs Losses and Bonds* exercise (4.2) can help you find that reason.

Identifying Obstacles

Most of us run into obstacles when we start pursuing our dreams. There is nothing abnormal about that—a dream that is worth giving you life *should* stretch you and force you to grow along the way. Obstacles come in two flavors, external and internal. External obstacles are circumstances that keep you from moving forward – things like a lack of money, skills or credentials. Internal obstacles are beliefs or thinking patterns that hold you back. If you believe that conflict is something to be avoided at all costs, for instance, you'll have a hard time dreaming about taking on roles or responsibilities that involve conflict.

External Obstacles

Get alone for a half hour or so and think about what external circumstances block the pursuit of a particular dream. It may help you to imagine moving toward your goal step by step. As you envision it, ask: "What do I need for this dream that I don't have and will be difficult to get?" The things you don't have but are confident you can acquire aren't obstacles—we're looking for the places you say, "I don't know how this could ever happen."

1. _____

2. _____

3. _____

4. _____

5. _____

Internal Obstacles

Now, imagine again the step-by-step journey of pursuing your dream from the beginning, and this time observe your *internal* reactions. How do you feel when you think of the different challenges your dream entails? Where do emotions like fear or doubt rise up? What is your inner critic telling you? Record your thoughts and feelings below.

1. _____

_____

2. _____

_____

3. _____

_____

When we think of pursuing our dreams, we usually have some idea of the costs and risks required to reach them. However, few people examine the cost of **not** pursuing a dream. This exercise helps you weigh the price of both courses of action.

Step 1: Get Into the Dream

This is an emotive exercise, and for it to work you have to really get into the dream. Visualize yourself living it. See it, touch it and experience that dream. What would be different in your life? How would it change you? What would it be worth to reach it? Going through the *Envisioning* exercise (8.4) can help.

Step 2: Look Back

Now, imagine that you are 75, looking back on what you've done in life. If you had never pursued this dream—the risk seemed too big, or you couldn't find the time or money—how would you feel about that?

- What would you lose?
- What would you think of yourself for making that choice?
- Would you be profoundly disappointed, or would it not be that big of a deal?

Step 3: Compare

Once you've gotten in touch with the cost of not pursuing your dream, compare it to the cost of going for it. How does this change the equation? What's the best long-term choice?

Chapter 10:
Passion/Values

"Lives based on having are less free than lives based on either doing or being."

William James

*T*he conflict between the two leaders was escalating fast. While they'd been putting the finishing touches on the travel arrangements for an extended mission trip, a disagreement arose over who should be included on the team. On a previous expedition, one younger team member had gotten homesick and left early, forcing a revamping of their plans. This time around, the team leader was firm: this trip was a crucial support for the new churches they'd planted, and they couldn't risk taking someone who'd bailed last time. His second-in-command was equally adamant: this young man had a big call on his life, and they needed to believe in him and get behind what God had created him to be. Finally, unable to resolve their differences, the two leaders parted ways.

This incident from Acts 15 is a values conflict between Paul and Barnabas over John Mark. Paul valued the task. Faithfulness and total commitment to the work are what he expected from team members, and those who didn't give their all needed to be replaced. Barnabas, the son of encouragement, valued developing people. He was the one who'd gone after Paul the outcast, brought him to Antioch and even stepped down from leading their first missionary journey to give Paul the opportunity to grow into his call. For Barnabas, developing people *was* the task. Unable to find a common ground on Mark, the two apostles parted ways.

As in this story, core values define our central Passions and form the basis of our decisions. Values have several shades of meaning:

- They are deeply held, enduring beliefs.
- Values define what is valuable or important to us in life.
- They are a framework for defining what we think is right and wrong.
- Values are understandings and expectations for how people ought to behave.

Values describe what we are most passionate about, what motivates us, and why we make certain choices. Values aren't aspirations about the future; they come out in everything we do *now*. If that seems a little fuzzy, you're not alone. Values are one of the tougher life purpose concepts to grasp. Here's an example of how a coach would help someone discover a value.

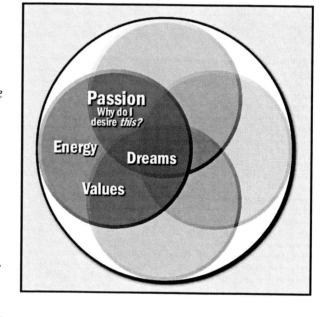

"I'm not sure I get this values thing. Can you describe that another way?"

"Sure, Nate. Would it help if we look at one of your own values?"

"That sounds good. I'm just not sure what they are."

"OK. Tell me about a decision you made recently—something you care about."

"Let's see… a couple of days ago I talked to my wife about supporting a child in Africa—you know, through Compassion International or something like that."

"And why do you want to do that?"

"Well, things have been pretty lean for the last five or six years. Between my wife quitting her job for the kids and starting the business, we've been stretched thin. But now the business is doing better, and we can afford to go beyond the bare necessities. I want to use some of what God has given us to bless others."

"And what's behind that, Nate?"

"It's caring for the least of these. It's doing the right thing. It's making sure that my finances don't just become about me."

"Why is that important to you?"

"Well, these are things that I believe in. And when you really believe in something, you do it. To say I want to live my life in the service of God and then just take all that He gives me for my personal benefit—I'd be a fraud."

"And why do you care about doing the right thing and not being a fraud?"

"That's what integrity is! It's doing what you say. And being a fraud is not doing what

you say."

"And what's behind integrity for you?"

"I just think, 'what kind of person are you if you don't have integrity?' I care about doing the right thing because it makes relationships work, or it's what makes the customers come back to my business, but even if it didn't bring in the business, I'd still do it. Integrity is its own reward."

"And that sounds like a value for you, Nate. We started with a decision, because values are the framework we make decisions by. I kept asking you why your rationale for giving was important, until you got down to the bedrock reason why you are doing it: integrity. You know you are at a value when you ask "why" and there is no more why. Like you said, integrity is its own reward."

"And that's why I do a lot of what I do, in all different areas of my life. OK, I think I'm getting it now."

To find a value, start with something significant and keep asking, "Why?" to dig down toward the underlying value. It may also help to compare what values are and aren't. The *Values Characteristics Worksheet* (10.1) gives examples of what is and isn't a value, and why.

> **Values Discovery Questions**
>
> - *"Why is that important to you?"*
>
> - *"What things, if they were taken away or you couldn't do them, would make life unbearable? What makes these things valuable to you?"*
>
> - *"When making your most important decisions, what are the fundamentals you base them on?"*
>
> - *"Where do you invest the best of your time, money and energy? Why?"*
>
> - *"What are your 'soap box' issues? Your deep concerns? Why?"*
>
> - *"What do you take the most pride in? What most excites you in life? Why?"*

Discovering Your Values

There are several types of value sets you can create. One option is to develop values around different sectors of life, like work, family, or spiritual life. The *Life Wheel Categories* (8.2) help you examine what motivates you in many different areas. One advantage of this approach is that you don't end up with a value set that covers only one part of life (like work or spiritual life). Plus, it is easier to identify and create values one area at a time than to try to cover everything at once.

A second option is a global set of personal values that apply to all areas of life. This is most suitable for people who are highly self-aware or who have done values work before. A third type of value set is *Leadership Values* (see 10.8). Focusing in on why you do what you do as a leader is tremendously helpful to an organizational or team environment.

To find a value, you start with something important and keep asking, "Why?" to push the conversation toward the underlying value. When you begin circling back around to the same idea over and over, you've reached the core value. Having a friend question you can be a good way to start finding values.

The *Values Brain Dump* exercise (10.2) will get you started. An example is given with values for two of the *Life Wheel Categories* (you would do all eight). You can do it either as a reflection or by having a friend ask questions. Another option is to use a word choice exercise (like 10.3) that lets you pick values words from a list. The word list is more limiting, but if you are stuck on the brain dump it will get you going.

Once you have a list of values words or jottings, the next step is grouping them into themes that will become the actual value statements (step 2 of the *Values Brain Dump* exercise). If you are creating statements around the life categories, at most two or three themes per category are enough. For a global value set, five to 10 total themes is a good number.

Finally, value statements in sentence form are developed out of these themes using exercise 10.6. A page of *Value Statement Examples* (10.7) is given to help guide you in this process. Limiting your list to a few values and wording them in pithy phrases makes your values more valuable—long, abstract statements filed away somewhere are of little use. When you are actually making decisions about life, you want your values at your fingertips. The four key things I look for in a final statement are listed on the bottom of the *Values Characteristics* worksheet (10.1):

1. **Short**: One memorable phrase or sentence is great. A cue word to remember the value by is also a big help. Rambling statements containing several different concepts should be edited down to what is most important.

2. **Unique**: Your own words. Something that has meaning for you. Not standard blasé lingo or other people's phrases.

3. **Unpack-able**: Every phrase has meaning. You can easily unpack what you've written to describe it in more depth.

4. **Now**: The value is written in present tense (i.e. "I value" instead of "I will"). It describes who you are, not what you want or will do.

Values Characteristics

Core values are deeply held, enduring beliefs that define what is most valuable or important to us. Below are a few characteristics defining what values are and aren't.

Values ARE:

- **Passionate.** They define what you care most about and why you do what you do.
- **Unique.** Since they come from your heart, they're in your own words.
- **Assumed.** Values are so much a part of us that we forget that they are there.
- **Lived.** If you truly value something, your behavior demonstrates it.
- **Lasting.** Values don't change easily—they're deeply rooted in you.

Values Are NOT:

- **Goals.** Goals are committed future aims. Values are what you hold dear now.
- **Aspirations.** A value is something you already live, not what you aspire to.
- **Principles.** Values are not cause and effect statements of how life works, like "You reap what you sow."
- **Doctrinal Statements.** "I believe the Bible is the inerrant word of God" is a doctrinal statement, not a value.
- **Visions.** Values are rooted in the now; visions are pictures of an ideal future.

Four Characteristics of Great Value Statements

1. **Short:** One sentence, one phrase, or even a single word to keep it memorable.
   - *"Now, can you sum that up in one sentence?"*
   - *"Can you shorten that into some pithy, meaningful phrases that can be unpacked?"*

2. **Unique:** In your words, not someone else's.
   - *"The language you are using could be true of a lot of people. Can you say that in a way that captures what is unique about you?"*
   - *"Can you say that in a way that if your friends read it they'd know it was you?"*

3. **Unpack-able:** Every word and phrase has meaning.
   - *"Unpack that for me—what does each phrase mean to you?"*
   - *"Take the key words there and tell me what each one means."*

4. **Now:** Written in the present tense, to describe who you are.
   - *"How well is this statement reflected in your life right now?"*
   - *"Is that a value that you are living out already, or is it something you aspire to that we might set a goal to reach?"*

This exercise can be done in two ways: either as a general brain dump to create a global set of values, or by using the *Life Wheel Categories* (Work, Money, Living Environment, Personal Growth, Health and Recreation, Community, Family, God—see also 8.2).

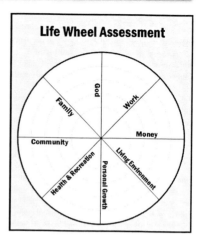

Life Wheel Assessment

Step 1: Brain Dump

Start with a stream-of-consciousness brain dump of words and phrases. What do you care most about in life? What's really important? Where do you invest the best of your time and energy, and why? What are the enduring priorities that drive your decisions? If you are using the eight categories, take each one in turn and brainstorm for five minutes or so in that area. Don't worry about organizing or evaluating your thoughts—at this point, you just need to get them down on paper

Step 2: Cull and Group

Now, take a step back and look at what you've written. Can you group your value jottings into five to eight overall themes? If you are using the eight categories, try to cull it down to two or three key phrases that best express your passion in each area.

From the following list, circle the words that resonate most deeply with you and best describe what is important to you. Once you've picked out the ones that appeal to you, write them out on a separate sheet of paper. Are there some that are similar or could be grouped together? See if you can cull your list down to the five to seven themes or groups of words which are the "best of the best" in describing what you are passionate about.

Integrity	Freedom	Relationship	Financial independence
Honesty	Exploration	Team	Stewardship
Genuineness	Creativity	Community	Frugality
Authenticity	Fun	Belonging	Overflow
Accountability	Artistic	Depth	Sharing
Do what you say	Spontaneity	Being known	Benevolence
Directness	Flexibility	Intimacy	Life-long learning
Sincerity	Knowledge	Commitment	Investment
Strength	The search	Friendship	Success
Character	Meaning	Communication	Recognition
Follow-through	Influence	Gentleness	Community involvement
Sacrifice	Truth	Compassion	Career advancement
Legacy	Passion	Caring	Efficiency
Family	Seeing the world	Emotion	Accomplishment
Marriage	Adventure	Spiritual life	Focus
Duty	Diversity	Health	Purpose
Honor	Travel	Devotion	Achievement
Heritage	Change	Passionate pursuit	Building
Responsibility	Movement	Worship	Leadership
Harmony	New challenges	Generosity	Mastery
Security	Opportunity	Service	Competence
Stability	Enthusiasm	Reflection	Precision
Peace	Starting things	Reaching out	Excellence
Home	Entrepreneurial	Evangelism	Planning
Thoughtfulness	Motivation	Changing the world	Being knowledgeable
Practicality	Progress	Hospitality	Principles
Nurture	Inspiration	Concern	Rationality
Love	Renewal	Integration	
Beauty	Healing	Making a difference	
Romance	Nature		
Volunteering	The outdoors		

A fun way to flesh out your values is simply to talk them through with a close friend. Having to describe what you value out loud clarifies thinking and makes it easier to put those values down on paper later. For this exercise, you'll need a good friend, family member or spouse who is willing to dialogue with you for a half hour or so on values.

Simply share your values one at a time, and then try to unpack each phrase and explain what it means. Ask your friend to mirror back to you what he or she hears, to make it is clear. Then discuss back and forth a bit. Give the person the questions below so they can draw you out. And make sure if you say a great line to jot it down!

- "What does the phrase _____ mean?"
- "Why is that important to you?"
- "What's the part of this that makes you different than every other Christian?"
- "Can you give an example of how that value influences your choices?"
- "What's one way you already live that out now?"
- "In all that you just said, what are the two most important phrases?"

Writing Value Statements  10.6

Creating value statements gives you a memorable, concise summary you can carry around in your head. The more accessible your values, the more useful they are! This worksheet provides space for creating one value statement.

Step 1: Review Definitions

Take a moment first and review the *Value Statement Examples* (10.7) and *Values Characteristics* (10.1) to get your objective in mind.

Step 2: Create Statements

Next, take each theme and create a phrase or one–sentence statement for that area. Start by jotting out the key words or phrases you want to include, then try different combinations until you get a statement you like. Most people experiment with several versions before they settle on one. The most important thing is that your values capture what **you** truly value.

Step 3: Create Statement Titles

Create a one-word (or *brief* phrase) "title" for each statement as a memory device.

#1 Key Value Words and Phrases

Trial Versions

Title:

Final Statement #1:

#2 Key Value Words and Phrases:

Trial Versions:

Title:

Final Statement #2:

#3 Key Value Words and Phrases:

Trial Versions:

Title:

Final Statement #3:

Value Statement Examples

Below are some representative examples of short value statements, plus three common values problems with examples of how to troubleshoot them.

Example Statements

- *"I believe in respect for the dignity of the individual."*
- *"I value meeting God everywhere: in nature, in circumstances, in people. It's about relationship, not rules."*
- *"People before projects."*
- *"The transparency that meets God as healer and not just protector."*
- *"Integrity: your word is who you are."*
- *"I value living in oneness in marriage—intimacy in conversation, unity in decision-making and sharing in calling."*
- *"Sacrificing to attain excellence inspires others and honors God."*

Problem #1: Rambling

"I value helping and empowering people to be their best and live their best lives, resourcing them to discover who they were made to be, and walking with them to fulfill that potential, because people are created by God and are of ultimate worth."

Problem: All the "ands" and redundancy will make this a killer to remember. Your values should be something concise you can carry with you.

Better: *"I value seeing people as God created them, of ultimate worth, and helping them fulfill that potential."*

Problem #2: Goal-Oriented

"I will spend my life empowering people to reach their human potential, and strive to become a great resource that helps them fully walk out their destiny."

Problem: This also sounds more like a mission statement (an ultimate task) than a value (why you do what you do). Values describe your motivations, not what you will do in the future.

Better: *"Human potential and helping people fully attain it."*

Statement #3: Not Unique

"Being a godly husband and loving my wife as Christ loved the church."

Problem: This statement is vague and not very personal. What are you uniquely passionate about in marriage? How can you make this personal instead of theological?

Better: *"The little acts of love and service that make every moment a romance."*

Organizational leaders greatly benefit from creating a separate set of values for how they lead.

Step 1: Brain Dump

Start by doing a brain dump on the questions below:

- "What are the four or five most crucial values that guide the way you lead?"
- "What are your non-negotiables as a leader?"
- "What guiding principles form the basis for your leadership decisions?"

Step 2: Check the List

Pick out just the items in this list that strike you as most important for the way you lead, and jot down words and phrases that describe your values in those areas.

1. The place of Scripture
2. Single vs. multiple leadership, teamwork, feedback
3. Decision-making process
4. Interfacing with the culture
5. Relationships and their value
6. Leadership style: empowering, directing, collaborating, etc.
7. Gifting and leadership
8. The poor, the outcast, the less-fortunate
9. Evangelism/missions/community involvement
10. Discipleship/spiritual growth/maturity
11. Authority
12. Training, leadership development
13. A leader's lifestyle
14. Servanthood
15. Roles: of lay people, women
16. Creativity, innovation, change
17. Unity, restoration, reconciliation, diversity
18. Truth, integrity
19. Excellence
20. Authenticity, openness

Step 3: Create Values

Use exercises 10.5 and 10.6 to turn your values notes into final statements.[2]

2　*Values-Driven Leadership* by Aubrey Malphurs is a great resource for leadership values.

Question 4: What Has Life Prepared Me For? (Preparation)

"I will prepare, and someday my chance will come."

Abraham Lincoln

When Moses fled into the desert with his tail between his legs, he thought his life purpose was finished. After identifying with his people and their plight, he immediately attempted to use his power position to seek their welfare. Wasn't he a son of Pharaoh's household, uniquely prepared as a man of destiny on their behalf? Alone of the Hebrews, he was born to rule instead of to slavery. He knew the palace customs, had access to Pharaoh, and knew the movers and the shakers in Egyptian society. Who else was better qualified to lead?

Moses probably had the finest education that Egypt could give, in everything from history and politics to generalship and personal combat. He was accustomed to power, and he leveraged what he knew. Moses almost immediately resorted to force to reach his goal. But when Pharaoh found out about his rebellion, Moses was forced to flee into exile with just the clothes on his back. What a come-down it must have been when the golden child realized the limitations of his personal power and natural abilities!

It's not clear what Moses' strategy for deliverance was, other than that it involved killing. Growing up amidst the palace intrigues, one might naturally assume than an armed revolt and overthrow of the Egyptian government (with Moses ending up in Pharaoh's throne?) may have been on his mind. But God had other plans, and sent him to an apprenticeship in the desert.

It would have been easy for Moses to assume that those were aimless, wasted years. He knew there was something in his heart about delivering the Hebrews. But if that was the goal, what was happening to him made no sense. As an exile that had lost his palace position, favor and access, everything that looked like it might make his destiny possible was gone. Then to trudge through the wilderness as a total nobody for 40 years, to be stripped bare of everything he thought he was and thought he could accomplish—was there still anything left for Moses but to herd sheep? You can see how beaten down he was at the burning bush. God returned and said, "Now is the time! Fulfill your destiny!" Moses didn't seem to have any trouble talking to God—in fact, I get the impression he was used to divine conversation. But Moses didn't believe in his destiny or himself. "I can't do this!" He wailed, citing excuse after excuse. "I'm a nobody! Who am I to stand before Pharaoh? The people will never believe that you are with me. I'm not a good speaker. Send someone else!" The man that God spent 40 years preparing as his chosen deliverer felt totally unprepared.

There is more going on here than just Moses being humbled (although that was important—it took God 40 years to make him "the meekest man who ever lived" before he was ready for his task). The problem was that *Moses did not see the connection between his preparation and his destiny,* because he was being prepared in a role outside his area of call.

Very often, God trains us in the skills and character our destiny requires in a place that seems totally disconnected from what we think we're supposed to do. Moses' struggle was intensified because his character preparation required *removing* him from a position very much like his ultimate role, and demoting him into a much smaller sphere of influence. Because Moses did not really understand what his destiny would require of him, or the ways of God in preparing leadership character, he did not recognize God's preparation for what it was.

Consider for a moment a few of the things Moses learned herding Jethro's sheep. Because he was destined to lead a group of slaves who'd lived along the Nile for 400 years, he was the only one of the Hebrews who knew:

- How to survive in the desert.

- Where the roads were and how to navigate through the trackless wastes.
- Where the springs and the oases were.
- Where the best grazing for the cattle was at different times of year.
- What desert plants could be eaten by people and animals.
- The wild animals found in the desert, and how to handle them.
- What the local customs were.
- Where the forts and guarded places were.

Somebody needed to have a desert survival skill-set if all those slaves were going to navigate that unfamiliar environment, and God chose Moses as that someone. Moses learned basic leadership and cultural skills first, in Egypt. He learned his practical desert skills at the same time as he was learning character—humility and utter dependence on God. In fact, everything in Moses' life, from the circumstances of his birth to his upbringing to his years tending sheep fed into his calling. *Moses' whole life prepared him for what he was born to do.*

What is Preparation?

Preparation is one of the four key areas on the life purpose diagram. It's the sum total of the experiences you have in life that make you ready for your destiny. Since God is actively preparing you *for* something, your significant experiences are also predictive of your life purpose. Studying what God has taken you through reveals themes and connections that point toward your call.

For instance, a common Preparation episode involves experiencing the lifestyle or the sufferings of those you are called to serve. When Christ came in human form He experienced every temptation we have to endure—that is why we can approach Him with confidence when we face difficulty. He knows what it is like to be human.

> *Moses' whole life prepared him for what he was born to do.*

In the same way, if you are called to serve those who have struggled in their marriages or who are on the fringes of society, expect that God will take you through your own experiences of marital conflict or being friendless and rejected. That common experience of suffering is what allows those you are called to serve to approach *you* with confidence.

When you fully enter into a convergent role in your area of call, you'll see how everything you've ever experienced and learned is being leveraged into your life purpose. Part of the great satisfaction of that season of life is realizing that all of your life makes sense, even when you didn't understand it at the time. Early in life, experiences of suffering and adversity are often a mystery. It is only later, after you have learned to trust God in things you don't understand, that you begin to perceive how He has intricately woven his purposes for you throughout every experience in life.

While the area of Design is about discovering your *nature*, Preparation inventories your *nurture*. It includes learned skills, qualifications and credentials, the network and the favor you've developed, and your best accomplishments (as well as your failures).

Your Preparation is what enables you to fully function in your Design. Without the character building Preparation of life experience, your Design won't accomplish much of lasting value.

Outside Preparation

An in-depth look at this area is most valuable for those whose Preparation is taking place *outside* of their area of call. Very often, God trains us in the skills and character our destiny requires in a place that seems totally disconnected from what we think

> *Preparation is what enables you to fully function in your Design.*

we're supposed to do. A full-time mom re-entering the workplace or a businessman called to missions are good examples. We tend to overlook the value of this Preparation because so much of it involves *inward character* instead of *outward skills.*

Another classic example of Outside Preparation is Joseph. After a whirlwind shower, a good shave (maybe the first in years), and cleaning the dirt out from under his nails, he was hustled out of the dungeon to stand in front of the King of Egypt. If you'd looked only at his resume, he would have seemed totally unprepared for that moment. He was a prison intern! But his character and wisdom were so evident that Pharaoh instantly trusted him and gave him the reins of the Egyptian economy.

How did Joseph gain the confidence and security to move directly from the gutter of society into his call as a national leader? The secret is that Preparation is more about inward growth than acquiring skills and credentials. Most of Joseph's outward Preparation (learning the language, becoming a good manager, mastering Egyptian customs) happened in Potipher's house. The incident with Potipher's wife that sent him to prison marked his graduation from an initial season of outward Preparation, and the beginning of an intensive time of inward growth. Outwardly, he was demoted (just like Moses) to a much lower position than he had before. Inwardly, he was right on course, and grew by leaps and bounds in humility, trust and dependence on God.

Leaders like Joseph who have larger-than-average Callings also tend to go through extraordinary shaking and stripping experiences early in life. Being falsely accused, working under an abusive leader or suddenly finding yourself leading in the midst of an organizational meltdown often indicate that God has tapped you for great influence. Now that's a counter-intuitive insight!

The heart of Preparation is embodying Christ in character qualities like dependence, trust, humility, love, and grace. Character development is so important because the eternal content of what people receive when you serve them is the Christ that is embodied in you—the act of service is just the channel. The true power of service is not that you fixed my roof when I was in the hospital (although that is certainly valuable). It's that someone actually cared enough about me to love me in a practical way. And so I receive the heart of Christ through your service.

Your skills channel your character. So the better your outward skills, the more people are impacted by what's in your heart. If you have great leadership skills but you are primarily motivated by a deep need for approval and an ambition to be famous, the lasting impact of even the "good" things you do will be the damage and disappointment caused by your mixed motives. Some leaders will stand before Jesus on the last day and say, "Lord, didn't we build great ministries in your name, and give lots of money to your cause, and help many people?" And Jesus will reply, "That was really all about you. I didn't have anything to do with it."

Negative Preparation Experiences

Negative Preparation is when failure, suffering or difficulty brings us unexpected gifts that launch us toward our destiny. God does things His own way—sometimes it is almost impossible to tease out what He is up to until He brings it all together. He must like surprises, or just the joy of seeing us go, "Wow!" when a wonderful part of our Passion arises out of what looked like a mistake.

> *Much of a leader's preparation focuses on character development, not just skills.*

For example, my basic Calling statement is "building leadership character and creating systems that build leadership character." A vital part of my Preparation happened outside my area of call, while I was working as a custom furniture designer. We were understaffed and overworked most of the time. Some of it was my own doing—I built our sales up to the point where I could barely handle the workload. There were times I hated the pressure cooker. Because so much had to be done, I became a master of minimalism. I sold $15,000 jobs from a ten-minute sketch on a piece of graph paper. I cut the average time to price a job from an hour to less than five minutes. Still, I was inevitably weeks behind schedule. Always delivering late and repeatedly disappointing the customers and craftsmen, I often felt like a failure.

At the time, I was just trying to do my job. I didn't see any connection between what I was going through and where I wanted to be (in ministry). All I knew was that God put me in that job and He hadn't given me the freedom to leave (not that I didn't ask Him every year to let me go!) Toward the end of that season of life, I began to wonder if I would ever get to do what I was called to. Like Moses, right at about the time when God was finishing up the Preparation was when I felt most stuck and abandoned by God.

It was only years later that I realized the incredible gift of that job: I learned to be highly creative and relentlessly productive whether I felt like it or not. A lot of authors struggle with writer's block, or feel like they have to have the right mood hit them before they can write. After 15 years of being forced to produce under pressure, that rarely bothers me. I know how to sit down and write, I know how to work to an achievable standard, and I know when to stop tweaking and say, "It's done." God used my job as a furniture designer to shape me for my call when I didn't even realize He was doing it.

Preparation Discovery

So how do you discover how God has prepared you? A good first step is to do the *Preparation Resume* (11.2). This straightforward inventory asks you to list things like educational credentials, job experience or important learnings you've picked up in life. If you are working outside your area of call, the *Outside Preparation* exercise

(11.3) can help you tease out the connections between your experiences and your destiny.

The *Internal Preparation Resume (11.4)* is a bit more difficult. It focuses in on where you have developed character in life. Since character is built in adversity, the *Negative Preparation* exercise (11.5) can help if you are drawing a blank. Take a look also at the *Preparation Principles* worksheet (11.1). This list of some ways God prepares leaders can help you tune into the significance of some of the challenges you've faced in life.

After you've finished your *Preparation Resumes,* the next step is often to create practical strategies for filling the holes in your resume. The *Outside Preparation* exercise (11.3) can easily be adapted to this chore. To take internal preparation a step further, the *Life Messages* exercise (14.1) restates the character qualities you identified in your Preparation as messages God has planted in you for others.

> **Preparation Discovery Questions**
> There are four basic questions to ask:
>
> 1. *"What have I **experienced**?"*
> 2. *"How are those experiences **valuable**?"*
> 3. *"How do those experiences give me practical **skills** for what I am called to do?"*
> 4. *"How have those experiences given me the **character** qualities I need to reach my destiny?"*

Preparation Principles

The best perspective questions come out of an understanding the principles of how God develops leaders. Below are a few examples of preparation principles that occur often in the lives of developing leaders:

- God will take you through experiences that help you identify with those you are called to serve. For instance, if you are called to minister to the grieving, your own grief will prepare you for that task.

- Many of your experiences build the faith and fortitude muscles you'll need to succeed in your calling. Dealing with the annoying people in your office builds the skills and character to deal with human needs on a larger scale.

- Failure is as good a preparation as success. If your calling involves revitalizing dying organizations, what better preparation than to be part of an organization that dies—or better yet, to lead one?

- Often God has to excise a lesser love in your life to make room for you to embrace His greater purpose. Having your company go belly up is an excellent way to become detached from pursuing material things.

- When God deals with a leader, everyone who serves under that person also gets dealt with. This adversity may be primarily about someone else's preparation. Are you willing to pay a price for their destiny?

- Your place of power in ministry is where God has most deeply dealt with your character—because that's where Christ is most fully incarnate in you. For instance, if you are called to teach leadership skills, expect God to put your own leadership under a microscope and hold you to an unfairly high standard compared to others.

- God often gives leaders a glimpse of their call early in life, but then there is a long season of inward preparation in relative obscurity before they emerge into that call. If you feel stuck in that middle season, it always helps to look at the time lines of Abraham, David, Joseph, Paul, or even Jesus for comparison.

- God will not allow you to enter your call from a place of security, where all your needs are met. Your destiny will require faith for God's provision.

- Big leadership challenges early in life can be an indicator of a large sphere calling.

- Graduating successfully from a certain stage of your Preparation is usually marked by removal from that sphere or facing a larger challenge. Endings don't mean you've failed. God wouldn't give it to you if He didn't think you were ready for it.

- A wilderness season is a mark of special affection from God. He leads us into the desert to draw us into deeper intimacy with Him (Hos. 2:14-16).

In this exercise, we're going to create a resume of the outward qualifications you've accumulated that prepare you for your life purpose. At this point, don't worry too much about connecting a specific qualification with your purpose—just list everything that falls under each category and we'll sort it out later.

1. Credentials

Degrees, certifications, education, awards and other recognized qualifications.

2. Accomplishments

What are your best accomplishments at work, in volunteer roles and at home?

3. Work/Life Experience

What major things have you experienced in life? What roles have you filled? What does your experience equip you to do, understand or communicate to others?

4. Network/Favor

Who knows you, and where do you have favor or opportunity through your relationships?

5. Skills

What skills have you acquired along the way? Where do you have expertise?

It is much easier to see how you've grown toward your call when that preparation happens within your area of calling. If you are a stay-at-home mom reentering the working world or a businessman transitioning to ministry, figuring out how your prior experience benefits you is tougher. This exercise helps you inventory the skills you've mastered outside your area of call and apply them to your destiny role.

Step 1: Inventory Learnings

Take each of the eight *Life Wheel Categories* (Work, Money, Living Environment, Personal Growth, Health and Recreation, Community, Family, God—see 8.2) and list the major life skills, competencies and character qualities you've developed in life (use the worksheet on the next page). What have you mastered? What skills have you picked up by working outside your area of call? What do you know that you didn't before? Put down significant life skills even if they seem unrelated to your destiny.

Step 2: Generalize into Competencies

The key to this exercise is identifying *general competencies,* not context-specific skills. The underlying general competencies in what you've done apply to anything—the context-specific part only happens in the particular role you were in.

> *Example: As a mom, you learned how to shop efficiently for groceries, keep to a monthly budget, do meal planning, and get the food on the table by 6:00 every night. Picking which brand of tuna to buy or finding the store with the best price on Pampers™ are context-specific skills—they go with the mom role. The general competencies are more interesting: you know how to manage time, stay within a budget, and maximize the efficiency of a task. Those skills have many applications!*

Step 3: Translate to Your Destiny Role

Now you're going to translate your generalized skills into your area of call. With a coach or a friend who works in your calling area, apply your general competencies to your destiny role. Where would you be doing similar things? How do the skills you've acquired give you a ready-made foundation to build on? What do you still need to learn to succeed in the new role?

> *Example: If you translate our mom's skills into business-speak, she's run a project on-time and on budget, met her deliverables and maximized the return on investment. She might need to learn to function this way on a larger scale, or in different areas, or gain the specific technical knowledge to apply her skills in a certain field, but the foundational project management skills are already in place.*

Outside Preparation (Worksheet)  11.3

1. What have I learned in my various roles?

2. What general competencies have I obtained? Which could apply to my destiny role?

Character isn't something you are born with—it is built through life experience. Every circumstance you face has the potential to prepare you for your destiny. In this exercise, we'll inventory the character-building experiences you've had and how they have shaped you.

1. Childhood

What character qualities were deeply instilled in you by your parents? Early lessons on things like truthfulness, hard work, sharing and respect can last a lifetime.

2. Roles

Reflect on different roles you've filled. What were the character lessons in each role?

3. Failures

What are the significant failures in your life? How have they shaped who you are?

4. Successes

Where have you applied yourself to do something with excellence? What character qualities were built in you through the pursuit of that goal?

5. Patterns

What patterns do you see in the way God is preparing you? In what areas has He worked on you repeatedly or held you to a higher standard? How do these patterns link to your destiny?

This exercise helps you understand how God is preparing you through the negative experiences in life.

Step 1: Life Purpose Review

Jot down a quick statement of your life purpose as you best understand it.

Step 2: Inventory

What are the major difficulties, failures or experiences of suffering you've gone through in life? Jot them down in the **left** column. Then note potential connections between those experiences and your life purpose on the **right** using these questions:

1. **Audience:** How did this experience draw me toward the needs of those I am called to? How might it give me opportunities to reach or serve them?

2. **Task:** What does this experience make me passionate about doing for others? What do I want to change or save others from because I went through it?

3. **Message:** How did this shape my identity? What message for others is implanted in the story of my life from going through this experience?

4. **Impact:** How will this experience make me more effective in my call?

Experience	Connection

Chapter 12: Preparation/ Destiny Events

*"It is with the heart that one sees rightly;
what is essential is invisible to the eye."*

Antoine de Saint-Exupery

You need to know something about your life purpose to figure out how you are being prepared for it. So how do you inventory your Preparation if you are drawing a blank about your purpose? And what does Preparation mean if you only became a Christian in mid-life—are the years before that wasted?

Sometimes you need a completely different way to see the destiny clues God has planted in your experiences. The *Destiny Events* exercise (12.1) is just such a tool.

A Destiny Event is a brief experience where we sense we are doing the kind of thing we were born to do. People often describe it as a time when they were "firing on all cylinders" or "doing something that brought out my best." These experiences are generally associated with:

1. A sense of **fulfillment**, significance and deep satisfaction.
2. Heightened **effectiveness** or exceptional impact.
3. Strong **affirmation** from others.

What we do is find the places where your own discernment says you were doing something similar to your life mission, tease out the details of those experiences, and then generalize (extrapolate) the details to into a picture of your destiny.

It is easiest to draw out the insights when the experience is a short, discrete event—a weekend workshop, a single conversation, a short-term project, or one business trip. When people talk about a sense of destiny around a role or longer project, they start to generalize and summarize, and that's not what we want. With *Destiny Events*, the insight comes from examining *specific details*. By going back to this original raw data, we can bypass any pre-existing conclusions about who we are and get a fresh picture of our destiny.

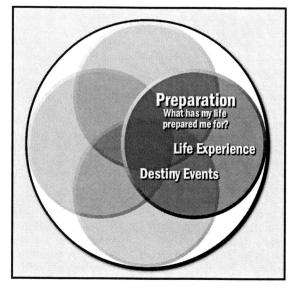

Here's an example of how a coach used the *Destiny Events* concept to take Randy past his obstacles and get him in touch with his Preparation:

"So, Randy—what I'm hearing is that you don't see any clues to your destiny in your past."

"Well, yeah. I mean, I didn't get saved until two years ago. Before that I pretty much wasted my life. When I wasn't partying, I was either sleeping off a hangover or just trying to make it through to the next weekend. I've got my life turned around now, but you won't find my call in my past—it's just a waste."

"OK. Let's try this: think of a time in your life when you were really clicking; when you were doing a project or task that came naturally and you felt you could really excel at."

"Nothing really comes to mind. I mean, I put together some major wild parties, but that's not the kind of thing that would be very useful now."

"Just bear with me here, Randy, and see where this goes—you can tell me if there is anything to it at the end. What was the biggest, most successful or most creative party you ever put together?"

"Well… there was the time I got most of the junior class together for a bash. There were 250 people there before the cops came."

"All right—tell me about that. Did you set it up?"

"Pretty much. I got all excited and talked a couple of my buds

The client discounts his B.C. (Before Christ) experiences as not related to his purpose.

Step 1: the coach asks for a destiny event without connecting it to purpose, but Randy's obstacle still blocks him.

The coach takes something Randy discounted and asks permission to draw out that story.

"Pretty much. I got all excited and talked a couple of my buds into helping. I put Brady in charge of posting it on FaceBook and letting everybody know. Deshawn got the beer from his Dad—he drives a Budweiser truck—and Reg held down the door and took people's money. He was the only one of us that could have a wad of cash in his pocket and not just blow it."

"What else did you do?"

"It was around Halloween, so we promoted it as a haunted house. What made it work was recruiting the captain of the basketball team to be the front man. If the parents knew it was my idea they'd have banned their kids from coming. Everything was going great until the neighbors got ticked off about the cars and the noise and called 911."

"Tell me more about the house."

"It was pretty cool—we got skeletons and flashing lights and all kinds of wild stuff. One girl actually fainted on the way through. Paul and I 'borrowed' some black lights from the art wing, and we did a lot with that. I found some girls from art class that were into painting weird animals and corpses and stuff—they were a little whacked out—and they made quite a show of it."

"So why did you go to all the work of doing a bash instead of just hanging out with your friends?"

"I guess I like including people—the more the merrier. I've always run with different crowds, and it seemed like a neat idea to try to get everyone to come. Hanging out in Reg's basement is no challenge—we could do that any time. I guess I wanted to make a mark."

"Great. Now, what I'm going to do is feed back to you what I heard that might connect with your life purpose, and you tell me if it is on target or not. First, you seem to be a natural leader and visionary. I would guess that your destiny involves rallying people around a big dream, recruiting a team like you did here, delegating tasks and catalyzing something big. You don't think small—you wanted the whole class to get together, and you managed to pull it off. Does that sound like you?"

"Well, I've never really looked at it that way. I guess it fits. I've always gotten other people involved in my schemes—got them in trouble as often as not. But yeah, I'm pretty good at organizing, recruiting and delegating."

"I also think it is significant that you understood where the favor was—with the basketball captain—and you were able to use it to allay the parent's concern. You seem to have a natural ability to size up the politics of a situation and plan accordingly. It is also interesting that you recruited a person of influence. You seem to have been a black sheep in your school days, but you

Step 2: The coach starts drawing out specific details.

The more details the better!

Drawing out details about inner motives…

Step 3: The coach generalizes the details into life purpose statements.

Step 4: Ask for the client to evaluation what you propose and tell you what of it is on target.

The coach generalizes a second set of details into purpose statements.

didn't just hang out with the Goths, either. Another good guess would be that your destiny will involve building bridges across cultural divides. I've seen you do that several times since we started meeting. So—what do you think, Randy? What of all that bears witness with you?"

"I guess a lot of it does. People sort of gravitate to me, and I've been able to get in with the fringe kids as well as the parents and the authority figures to do stuff with the youth group. It comes so natural I never really thought of it as something special."

"You are exceptionally gifted in some of these areas."

"So what you are saying is that I learned how to be a visionary while I was still in the world, and now God is going to use that experience for His Kingdom?"

"Randy, the same natural strengths and abilities you used to organize parties are the ones you'll use for God. He's not about giving you a personality transplant—He's redeeming your life. All of it."

"Wow. That's amazing."

The client begins to make the missing connections between these experiences and his calling and design.

Randy had lived on the wild side before he gave himself to Christ. Because he saw his life before Christ as "wasted," identifying the Preparation in his life story wasn't part of Randy's paradigm. To bypass this obstacle, the coach employed the *Destiny Events* technique[3].

The main steps of the process are, first, identify a destiny event; second, draw out as many specific details as you can remember about that event; and third, generalize or extrapolate those details into life purpose insights.

The step of making generalized purpose statements always feels risky. Essentially, you are taking a single piece of data and extrapolating it to your entire life! What makes the technique work is that you've sorted through literally thousands of experiences and picked the ones where you have the greatest sense of being in your destiny. Because you've sorted so precisely for best-fit experiences, the seemingly-random details become exceptionally significant. Believe that there is meaning in the details, and you'll be amazed at the connections that pop out.

Destiny Events Technique

1. Identify destiny events
2. Draw out details
3. Generalize details into life purpose statements

---

3   The Destiny Events concept draws from ideas first popularized by Doug Fike under the name "Mini-convergences."

Destiny Events

Recruit a spouse, friend or coach to help you do this exercise.

Step 1: Identify Destiny Events

Destiny Events are experiences where you felt totally in the zone: fulfilled, effective, and aligned with your call. Identify three of these experiences where you felt you were doing what you were born to do, doing it well, and having a great impact. Think of *specific, discrete events:* something that happened in a day or a week, NOT a role you filled or a longer season in life.

Step 2: Draw Out the Details

Take 10 to 15 minutes to identify as many specific details as you can remember about each experience. If possible, recruit a good friend or your spouse to ask questions like the ones below. Jot down possible connections between those details and your destiny as you see them on the worksheet (next page).

- "Exactly what happened? Walk me through the experience, step by step."
- "Who did you serve? What impact did you have on others?"
- "What kind of task were you doing? How did you do it? What was accomplished?"
- "What else can you remember?"

Step 3: Generalize/Look for Themes

Compare your three stories using the following questions. Since we sorted out events with a high sense of destiny, the details can give an amazingly accurate picture of your life purpose (especially when they pop up repeatedly). If you generalized these repeated themes into statements about your life purpose, what would they say?

- "What's a common element in all these stories? What does that tell you?"
- "Is there a message you have for others that comes up repeatedly in these experiences?"
- "What do the people you served in these three stories have in common?"
- "What strengths or gifts are you drawing on in all these events?"
- "It was interesting to me that _____ [cite a detail that caught your attention]. How might that connect to your life purpose?"

Significant Details

Connections Between Details and Destiny

Destiny Event Themes

Question 5: Where is the Master Sending Me? (Calling)

"Go forth from your country, and from your relatives and from your father's house, to the land which I will show you; and I will make you a great nation... in you all the families of the earth will be blessed."

Genesis 12:1-3

When Israel asked for a king, God honored their request and gave them one. He spoke to Samuel the prophet: "...and you shall anoint him [Saul] to be prince over my people Israel; and he will deliver my people from the hand of the Philistines. For I have regarded my people, because their cry has come to me" (I Sam. 9:16). Saul's calling task was to lead God's people and save them from their enemies (I Sam. 10:1).

When the Bible lists Saul's qualifications, the focus seems to be on outward appearances. He was the tallest and most handsome of all—the rock-star method of leadership selection. The people were very taken with their physically-imposing king—whom they then discovered hiding in the baggage to escape his call! Apparently what was on the inside was less important to them than looking the part. You get the sense that God was saying, "It wasn't *my* idea for you to have a king, but since you asked for one, here's a man that fits *your* criteria."

The call of David has a completely different flavor: "...The Lord has sought out for Himself a man after his own heart, and the Lord has appointed him as ruler over his people..." (I Sam. 13:14). In the process of recognizing this king, Samuel got an impromptu lesson on the leadership qualities God prefers. When Samuel set eyes on tall, handsome, first-born Eliab, God warned, "Do not look at his appearance or the height of his stature, because I have rejected him; for God sees not as man sees; for man looks on the outward appearance, but the Lord looks at the heart" (I Sam. 16:7).

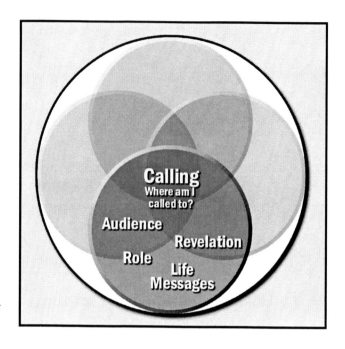

These two different emphases are at the heart of why Saul's kingship was a failure. Even though he largely accomplished his Calling *task* (or life mission— the doing part of his call) of delivering Israel from their oppressors, Saul never embodied the heart of his call—modeling God as King (the being side of call). His failure to become the man he was called to be eventually cost him the people's hearts, the throne and his life.

David, by contrast, was a great success in the message part of his call: being "a man after God's own heart." David's story and his Psalms preserve a record of his victories and failures, his rejoicing and repentance, and his wrestling with God. We even get a window into David's lifelong struggle with vengeance, from the heights of refusing to raise his hand against Saul to the depths of telling Solomon on his death bed to be sure and take care of his old enemies.

David was not a perfect man. The message of his life is not about doing it right, but about bringing all of the human heart—passion, desire, emotion, identity, self-image, failure, success—to God. David was a man after God's own heart because everything in his heart was brought to God—he embodied engaging God at the deepest level.

The Four Facets of Call

Calling is an external commission from God for others. David's life is an excellent example of the being/doing tension in call. That tension is expressed in the Four Facets of Calling:

> Calling is…
> A **message** you embody
> To a specific **audience**
> For an ultimate **impact**
> Through a unique **task.**

You have a life **Message** that impacts others as you do your life task. It's the unique way Jesus shines through you because of how He has shaped your identity. Here's an example. Years ago some good friends discovered their unborn child had a heart deformity and almost certainly wouldn't survive. Instead of getting an abortion, they prayed fervently through the full term, went through the birth, and then watched their child die a few days later. It was a heart-wrenching experience putting that tiny coffin in the ground on a lifeless winter day.

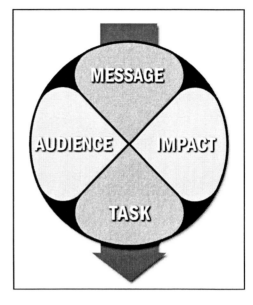

That couple went through the pain with Jesus and came out whole. If I ever run into someone who's enduring the death of a baby, that's where I'd send them. Because they met God in their suffering, this couple embodies a message to others in that valley of death.

The message of your life is rooted in the places God has deeply dealt with you, not in your natural strengths or what comes easily. Opening yourself to allow Christ to engrave His message on your heart is the heart of your call. It's not the outward task that accomplishes God's purpose, but the impartation that comes *through* the task—like the message of David's hunger for God that shines through every time we read the Psalms.

Your life message resonates with certain people—your **Audience**. Those you are called to need exactly what God has put into your heart. Your Preparation uniquely qualifies you to speak to them, and makes you the kind of person they'll listen to.

The reason for all this is to create an **Impact** on those lives. Your legacy is the ultimate impact of your life message on your target audience, reverberating down through the generations. A true call is never just to build an organization or complete a project—it is to serve real people *through* the organization or project.

The **Task** your message flows through is also crucial. You have a unique life mission that is the most effective conduit for your message. That task is what puts hands and feet to the Christ-in-you and connects Him to your audience. There are certain roles that best fit your Design and express your heart. The task without a message is empty; but without the proper channel of an appropriate task or role, your message is limited and ineffective.

We'll delve into all four of these areas, starting with the concept of revelation (how you receive your call). Then we'll explore your message, audience, and impact, and the task those three things are channeled through. Finally, we'll discuss best-fit roles for your life task.

Misconceptions and Reality

What do you think it would look like to receive a call? The classic picture is a young man, kneeling in a grove to pray for direction for his life. Suddenly, a light flashes around him (or an almost-audible voice speaks) and God gives him an unmistakable call to the ministry. Or a girl sits listening on Sunday night to a missionary, back on furlough with videos of destitute villages in Africa. Something stirs in her heart, and she goes up to the altar and receives a call to serve the less fortunate on the mission field.

Unfortunately, this picture contains three big misconceptions that often keep us from recognizing how God has called us. First, we assume that our call is to a *task*—call is something you do. I was on the phone yesterday with a young pastor in a self-described "leadership funk." He was not accomplishing what he hoped to, and felt bogged down, guilty and frustrated. I began challenging him to look at things from a different perspective. "What if God is in the fact that you aren't accomplishing much right now? What if God *is* answering your prayers, but the road to changing your church begins by changing *you*, not your circumstances?"

The lights came on when he began to tune into God's agenda for his inner growth and not just for getting his tasks done. When we think of Calling solely in task terms we get all tied up in knots about doing the right thing and finding God's will. When the focus is on embodying Jesus as our call, much of that performance anxiety disappears.

A second misconception is that when you find your call, you are supposed to just start doing it, right now. If I am called to run an organic farm or to help foster kids as a social worker, I need to find a position in those fields right away. Once I know my call, any time I spend doing something else is wasted.

The reality is much different. Preparation usually takes decades, not just years, and it is common for God to do much of that preparatory work in an unrelated field. Remember that Jesus was prepared for His ministry call by doing manual labor as a carpenter. There is a season of life (normally 40's at the earliest) to enter your destiny role and fulfill your call, and there is a season to focus on Preparation instead of production.

Misconceptions about Call

1. A call is one special moment when God gives me a life assignment.

2. My calling is to a task.

3. Once I figure out my calling, I'm supposed to just start doing it.

Third, most people think of Calling as a special, dramatic, one-time *event* where God gives them a specific lifetime assignment. We're so locked into the idea of calling events that Christians who can't identify that one special moment feel like second-class citizens. But for most people, Calling is actually revealed *progressively* over time instead of through a single event. When we expect a dramatic call and it doesn't happen that way, it can be very disconcerting.

One reason we expect an extraordinary call is that there are lots of dramatic calling stories in the Bible. Are we too spiritually wimpy to get that kind of clear call, or do those stories simply represent the most memorable high points of 2000 years of Hebrew history? One objective way to find out is to look at the callings of a group of people instead of single, cherry-picked examples. The 12 disciples are a good test group. Each had very different experiences. Peter, James and John were amazed at the great catch of fish, and in that supernatural moment Jesus asked them to follow (in another version, they are called while sitting on the beach mending nets). In Matthew's case, Jesus just happened along the road one day and invited him to become a follower—not much drama there.

Andrew (Peter's brother and John the Baptist's disciple) went after Jesus when John pointed him out as the Lamb of God. He was a referral disciple. They met again while Peter and Andrew were fishing on the seashore, and Jesus told them to follow. I don't think that qualifies as the kind of supernatural event many people expect.

Jesus "found" Phillip one day and said to him, "Follow me." Apparently that was enough for Phillip—again, not too dramatic. Phillip then went and recruited his brother Nathaniel to come along—and Jesus named his inner identity and shared a vision of him under a fig tree. That supernatural insight so impressed Nathaniel that he was on board after just one meeting.

We only have stories of half of the 12. Of those, roughly half are dramatic and half less so. I would guess that the stories that got in the Bible would tend toward the more dramatic rather than the everyday ones. For instance, from Jesus' early life we have one dramatic story of Him amazing the temple priests with His insights, but none of His everyday work as a carpenter. So for half to three fourths of the 12 disciples, the call came through everyday conversations and circumstances instead of miraculous events. If that was true for Jesus' own disciples, I'd say it's a pretty safe bet that for the majority of us, God's call will not be attended by angelic visitations, audible voices or miracles.

The MapQuest Paradigm

Once you have an idea of what your call is, there are additional obstacles you may face on the journey to follow it. Some see following the call as akin to tiptoeing through a minefield. One false step and it's over—you've missed your call, and everything blows up in your face. I call this the *MapQuest Paradigm*. In this way of thinking, pursuing a call is like following a list of turn-by-turn directions from MapQuest.com. If you haven't used MapQuest yet, you go to the web site, type in the starting point and the destination, and it gives you back a complete list of each turn you need to make to get there.

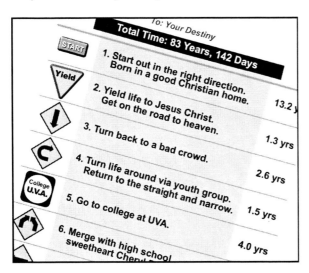

The thing I hate about MapQuest directions is, if you miss a turn you can pretty quickly get *totally lost*. (That's why I always print out the map, too.) A simple turn list doesn't help you visualize the twists and turns of the road, or show which compass direction you should be heading at a given moment, or give you any landmarks en route. It's a sick feeling to realize that you missed a turn somewhere 20 miles back (especially at night) and you have no idea where you are.

That's how many Christians operate. Each decision in life is a turn. There is a right and a wrong choice to make at each fork in the road, and you have to get all the turns right to reach the destination. If at some point you take a major wrong turn (like bankruptcy, divorce or coming to Christ later in life), you are lost, and so is your destiny. In the MapQuest paradigm, there is no way to get back on the highway once you miss a turn—you've missed God. Certainly, seeing every choice in life as a chance to screw up is a recipe for living a fearful, tentative life.

However, if you have an actual map you travel by instead of just a list of turns, you can find many ways to get to the same destination. You can even make a wrong turn or change your mind along the way and re-plan your route on the fly. There may be one way that is faster or more direct than the others, but the scenic route will get you there just the same.

The map image provides a much more accurate picture of Calling, because a map lets you base your route on principles ("interstates are faster than county roads") instead of just blind adherence to a set of rules. Following your call is as much about knowing the ways of God (the principles) as it is being in the right place at the right time (the turns).

The MapQuest paradigm is a pre-Christ worldview: grace and redemption are not part of the picture. But with grace, there is always a future and a hope. No matter where you are starting from, *today* (and each day) God will take your life and make something great of it.

Still wondering if maybe you have been disqualified by your failures? Let's look at the Bible. Did you feel called to deliver people from some suffering but ended up in business for the last 20 years instead? Maybe you and Moses ought to have a heart-to-heart—he's got 40 years in business to your 20. Had an affair with a friend's wife and destroyed your ministry along with your friendship? David dealt with God and became a better man for it—why can't you? Ashamed of how much you did in your pre-Christian years to turn people away from God? Maybe you and Paul should compare stories. If these leaders can walk through catastrophic failures and still go on to fulfill their destinies, what about you? God is still in the redemption business, and all you have to do to become a customer is to say, "Yes."

Calling is not primarily about the destination—it is about the incarnation.

The One True Destination

One final Calling trap is thinking that there is one right *destination* as well as one right route to get to it. There is only one place I must live that will suffice, one right job role to fill, or one particular project to complete to fulfill my life call. That kind of thinking gets you tied up in knots. I've worked with several individuals who felt God had shown them the one right person they were called to marry—and then that person went off and hitched up with someone else! What do you do with that?

Is there just one certain role in a particular town with a certain organization doing exactly one thing that represents your call? In short, no. *Calling is not primarily a destination—it is an incarnation.* The call is to embody something of Christ (being). The task (doing) is only the channel. You can be your call through everything and anything you do.

But it goes even further. At any moment, God takes whatever you are and works with you to make the most of it. If you choose course "A," He will take whatever that makes of your life, roll it into your call and work to maximize it. If you choose "B," He will do the same thing. *Calling is not a static, predetermined destination, but a dynamic, adaptive journey.* God actively recalibrates our Calling after each choice to take into account what He has to work with. We are partners with God in our life purpose. Our choices shape the plan and the destination—and yet all was foreknown by a God who stands outside of time and sees all days as one.

From a human perspective, God continuously adapts our call to our choices. From a divine one, he foresees every choice and his plan accounts for it. The mystery of receiving a call from a God who is outside of time is complicated.[4] However, the practical application is simple: we do the best we can to follow the best we know of our call, assured that God is working with us to make things turn out the way He desires.

> *Calling is not a static, predetermined destination, but a dynamic, adaptive journey.*

Abraham's life is a good example of a dynamically shaped Calling. When God called Abraham to "go to the land that I will show you," the promise was to "this land." When Abraham separated from Lot and let go of his inheritance instead of trying to make it happen, God appeared again, and told him that all the land in sight in all directions would be his. Then, after Abraham rescued Lot from the warring kings and refused to take the spoils of Sodom (another good choice), God reappeared, promised him the land from Sinai to the Euphrates, and named nine additional tribes his descendants would dispossess.

See the pattern here? As Abraham obeyed and grew in character, the revelation and scope of his call grew with it. God adjusted Abraham's call on the fly based on his choices (again, keeping in mind that we are describing this from a human perspective). Obedience expands your destiny.

Revelation Discovery

Revelation can come through dramatic events, everyday circumstances, or it can be an insight that develops progressively over a lifetime. When we use the word

---

4   I'm using the idea of human and divine perspectives to keep us from getting hung up on free will versus pre-destination. God dwells outside of the river time, in the timeless; so from His perspective, every moment happens in front of the same spot on the riverbank. We flow by in time, but He stands still and sees all. For the great I AM, there is no past or future—everything is now. But from a human perspective, each moment is new and unforeseen. We make choices about the direction our lives will flow, and our future is the product of those choices. Free will and predestination coexist with no intrinsic conflict—it's a matter of our frame of reference.

"revelation" as coaches, we are referring to all three. Two general categories of revelation are *Calling Events* (specific experiences we've been called through), which can be dramatic or everyday happenings; and *Progressive Revelation* of call, where we gradually come to understand our destiny over a period of years. For instance, Abraham received a series of calling events over a period of 25 years that put together progressively revealed his calling. The *Twelve Revelation Methods* worksheet (13.1) shows a variety of ways people report receiving a call. Take a minute and scan it before you read further.

The place to start your search for revelation is the *Revelation Journal* (13.2). This exercise helps you collect what God has spoken in a variety of ways. Make sure and reference the different *Revelation Methods* (13.1) as you do it so you don't miss something important.

One calling method that we often don't examine is inheritance and communal calls. While it is common in eastern cultures to understand one's call in the context of community or inheritance, western cultures ignore it in their emphasis on the individual. But since a call from God is always part of a much larger plan, often it

> ### Rethinking Failure
> Do you think you have failed or been unfaithful to your call? Here are some questions to ask:
>
> - *"If God redeemed your call like He redeemed your life, what would that mean?"*
> - *"God doesn't wipe away all the consequences of your failures. Let's say you have to deal with some lasting fallout from this. How might God weave that suffering into your call?"*
> - *"What life message might come from this failure?"*
> - *"If you started fresh now, and didn't worry about what was behind, what could you accomplish with your life?"*

is entwined with the larger story of one's family or community. For instance, many families have a heritage of generations of involvement in pastoral ministry, the military, a family business or a family farm. That family story can exert a strong influence on children. Or a family may have deeply held values (like higher education or community service) that influence the next generations' sense of what is significant. Some individuals, like Abraham's descendants, find their personal destiny in being part of a family call that spans generations.

Tapping into family and community heritage can be a crucial part of Calling discovery, especially for those from Asian backgrounds. We've included an inheritance section in the *Revelation Journal*, plus a *Family Calling Interview* exercise (13.3) to help you explore your family's sense of call.

If you felt called to something and it didn't work out, the *Lost in Translation* exercise (13.4) can help. Sometimes the imagery we put around what God says to us (He speaks in the spirit, we translate it into words) doesn't quite reflect what He actually said. This exercise takes you back to recapture the original call and separate it from your interpretations.

Here are 12 common ways people experience hearing a call from God.

1. **Drawing to a Need**
   I see a person, group, or need my heart is drawn to serve, and through that feel a larger sense of calling to meet those needs long-term (Moses).

2. **Personal Suffering**
   My call grows out of a personal experience of suffering and what is birthed in my heart through it (Job).

3. **Personal Success**
   God speaks to me through my success or overcoming something with a realization of what I can do on behalf of others (David, with Goliath).

4. **Demonstration of Gifting**
   My calling is demonstrated (and often recognized by others) through unusual or early manifestations of gifting or ability (Joseph).

5. **Childhood Dreams**
   God implants significant insights about the future in the hearts of children (Samuel).

6. **Holy Discontent**
   I can't stand something that is going on, and in the process of working against that injustice I discover my calling (Nehemiah).

7. **Inheritance/Community**
   My call comes through being part of my family, tribe or community, and embracing that group's sense of collective call (Isaac, Jacob, or Ruth).

8. **Affirmation/Confirmation**
   God uses others to name, confirm, or prophetically reveal my calling to me (David).

9. **Scripture**
   God reveals my call through a Scripture that is brought to life for me (Josiah).

10. **Circumstances**
    I find myself in a place of destiny where circumstances force me to respond (Esther).

11. **Direct Revelation**
    God speaks directly through an inner witness, dreams, visions or other supernatural means (Paul, Mary).

12. **Progressive Revelation**
    God uses many events, circumstances and insights to progressively unfold my call over a period of years (Abraham).

Record here what God has revealed to you about your call throughout your life. Keeping a running revelation journal is a great habit to develop!

Eureka Moments

Ever had an experience where everything came together and you felt you were doing what you were born to do? That's an inner witness that you are in your area of call. Jot down these experiences and what you think they tell you about your calling. (Look back at your responses in *Destiny Events* (12.1) if you completed that exercise.)

Direct Revelation

What has God directly spoken to you about your call, through His inner voice, words, dreams, or visions? What do you have an inner witness to pertaining to your call? Be bold about what you think you've heard. Even if you aren't certain, write it down here as something to look at.

Revelation Journal (cont'd)

Affirmation/Confirmation

What has God spoken to you through the people around you? If you've received strong affirmation in a gift or skill, someone you respect has named who you are, or you've received an important word or Scripture from someone, put it down here.

Key Scriptures

What key verses has God given you concerning your destiny? Is there a passage you are repeatedly drawn to because it expresses the essence of who you are and what's in your heart? Record those verses and the purpose insights that go with them here. Check your margin notes in your Bible or old journals if you need ideas.

Childhood Dreams

Sometimes God speaks clearly to children about their future, even when they don't know it is Him. What did you want to be as a kid? What did you want to do when you grew up? Who did you want to be like? Jot those items below, and if you can, identify what attracted you to that role. Don't get hung up on the outward role or the image ("I want to be a fireman"). Instead, look for what in that role that attracted you.

Design, Passion and Preparation

Take some time to go back and review the exercises you've done in the areas of Design, Passion and Preparation. Are there things you wrote down that are more than personal insights—that you sense are direction from God? Jot them down here.

Inheritance/Community

Think about your family, community and other groups you strongly identify with. What part of your call has been passed down to you (i.e. a family business, farm or lineage in a certain profession)? What strong values and traditions from your community or family influence your sense of call? How does your heritage make you part of a larger calling? (Exercise 13.3 can help you flesh this out.)

Revelation Summary

Once you've finished each category, step back and look it over. What are the common themes? What jumps out at you? Summarize what revelation tells you about your destiny.

This exercise identifies aspects of call that are passed down through generations in your family. Interview your parents or grandparents about your family heritage, using the questions below (they use terms like "story" and "vocation" that most people are comfortable with instead of "calling"). If an interview isn't possible, simply answer the questions yourself from what you know of your family history.

Family Vocation

- *"What professions did your parents, grandparents and great grandparents enter?"*
- *"What did your family most value vocationally?"*
- *"Does our family have a history of entering a certain profession? What's behind that?"*

Family Story

- *"What's our family story? What have we contributed to society through the generations?"*
- *"Is there one particular patriarch or matriarch whose story has defined our family heritage? What is that story?"*

Family Values

- *"What are you most proud of in our family history?"*
- *"What part of your heritage do you most value? What parts do others in the family value?"*
- *"What do you think your parents felt was most important to pass on to you? What was most important to you to pass on to your children?"*

Your Vocation

- *"How do you feel God has led you in what you've chosen to do with your life?"*
- *"What have you done vocationally that most felt like what you were made to do?"*

Your Message

- *"What is the message you most wanted to come through your life to others?"*
- *"What was unique about the way you did your job? How did you express who you were through it?"*

Part II: Interview Learnings

- "What were the most important insights into your heritage you got from this interview?"
- "How have your family's vocational choices and values impacted your sense of call?"
- "How is your family calling expressed in your own sense of call?"

Lost in Translation

A call is revealed by God to our spirits but is interpreted through our minds—and sometimes things get lost in translation. This exercise will help you record a calling experience or separate the substance of a calling event (exactly what God said) from the image you used at the time to understand or remember what was revealed.

Step 1: Record Current Understanding of Call

Sketch out the call you received in this calling event as you currently understand it. Is there an image or analogy you've used to describe it? Is there a certain task or role that seems to be "it?" Record your current images and expectations to whatever degree of clarity you have.

Step 2: Go Back to the Beginning

Next, try to write down *exactly the words or impressions you received from God* during the actual calling event. Try not to add anything—what *exactly* did God say to you, and how did He say it? What was the impression? What words did you hear or images did you see? Recapture as much as you can of that original moment.

Step 3: Fact Check

Compare the two versions of your call. Some changes may be due to additional progressive revelation since you received it—that's OK. Look for assumptions you made about the original that might differ from what was revealed or no longer fit.

Step 4: Evaluate

If you found some differences, step back and brainstorm with your coach. What other scenarios could fit what God said? How has your human interpretation of God's call limited your options? Is the image or container you've placed around your call still a good fit?

Chapter 14: Calling/Life Messages

"The will is transformed by experience, not information."

Dallas Willard

The core of Calling is incarnation—Christ becoming a message embodied in your heart. The word incarnation means to "enflesh"—to make something inward or invisible visible through your life. I call this embodiment a *Message* because it is the underlying meaning that impacts others through what you do.

A while back I was teaching on this subject and asked the group for examples of events that had deeply shaped them. One older woman spoke up and said, "The death of my husband." Certainly, that's a major shaping event! So I asked, "If you wouldn't mind sharing, how did you meet Jesus through that experience of suffering?" Without hesitation, she replied, "He became my husband. I learned to depend on Him totally, for everything. My Jesus became so precious to me through that time."

Wow. Imagine the impact of this woman, who has walked through that place, ministering to others who have lost a loved one (which is what God has her doing now). That's the kind of message that can transform lives.

Life Messages become part of us—they are permanently seared into our souls through significant experiences where we meet God and are transformed. For instance, Martin Luther's key life message was grace. As a young man, he was deeply convicted and morbidly guilty. Priests reportedly fled from the confessional booth when Luther appeared, because he was in the habit of confessing every sin he'd ever committed from childhood on—sometimes for four or five hours at a stretch!

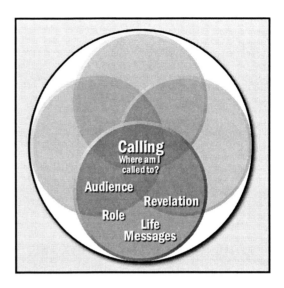

When the concept of grace finally penetrated Luther's heart, it turned his inner world upside down. The power of the Protestant Reformation grew directly out of the depth of God's work in his heart. Luther engaged God profoundly, to the depths of his soul, and the force of that encounter is directly proportional to the power of his message. God met him powerfully, and he was so transformed that grace was radically embodied through him for others. That's the most common life message pattern.

St. Francis of Assisi had a life message of renouncing all to have all of Christ. When he left his rich upbringing for the life of a monk, he actually stripped himself of all his expensive clothing, left it with his father and walked out naked into his new life. The impact of his life message down through the ages emerges directly out of being ripped free from encumbrance to the world and embracing utter dependence on God.

These are good pictures of how life messages form. Since incarnation is Christ worked deeply into our character, it is developed in the character-building situations we often wish we could avoid: practicing discipline, suffering, failure, challenging circumstances, or iron sharpening iron in relationships. When we encounter these shaping events, do the hard work of meeting God in them, and allow the character of Christ to be truly embodied there, we've created a place of power in our lives. Whatever we speak or do out of that part of our heart has exceptional impact on others.

Finding Life Messages

1. Identify a significant shaping event.
2. Identify the impact of meeting God in it.
3. Distill into a message.

Life Message Discovery

Life messages form where something deeply touched you, so you find them by identifying significant shaping events where God has dealt with your core being. Whenever you go through a life-changing occurrence you are experiencing potential life message material. You win your destiny in those moments! The *Life Messages* exercise (14.1) identifies these events in your life story and mines them for messages.

An alternate way to find life messages is by pinpointing the things you speak passionately about now, and using that as a jumping-off point to go back to the life experience that passion sprang from. The *Life Messages in Action* exercise (14.2) takes that approach, using indicators like "Soapbox Issues" (see box on next page) to pinpoint potential messages. *Confirming Life Messages* (14.3) is a peer validation exercise you can use to get feedback on your messages.

The *Calling through Suffering* exercise (14.5) keys in on different ways suffering and adversity grow into life messages. Most life purpose discovery tools look for destiny in the things that energize you and give you joy, which is legitimate. But many individuals find their sense of call comes as an unexpected gift in an experience of suffering. Six common calling patterns associated with suffering are:

- Confronting injustice you and I now suffer.
- Preventing you from suffering what I have suffered in the past.
- Being drawn by compassion to alleviate others' suffering.
- Earning a platform through suffering to address a need (qualification).
- Overcoming difficult circumstances and helping others overcome.
- Adapting to or accepting adversity with grace.

Sometimes individuals who don't have much to say on the *Revelation Journal* exercise can find their life purpose here.

The Message of Your Life

There's a special life message that's a summary of your story—the place where your various life messages join together in one theme. What one message does Jesus convey most clearly through your story? What is the central impartation that animates everything you do for others? That one-of-a-kind *Message of Your Life* (14.4) is the heart of your call. It's your life purpose in being terms, the thing that you must embody to fulfill your destiny.

For example, some of my life messages are authenticity, dealing with God, meeting God in suffering and adversity, transformational change, Sabbath rest, and grace instead of legalism. The central theme (as best I understand it) that's the message of my life is, "You can meet God in anything, especially suffering and adversity, and be transformed." That explains this book's emphasis. I didn't write an encouraging, follow-your-bliss book about the adventure of living your destiny, because *that's not the message of my life.* I have the greatest impact on others when I am imparting my core message of heart transformation.

The message of Abraham's life was justification through faith. The Bible calls Abraham a "father of faith" because he was the first person to figure out that believing in God and walking in that faith was what God was really after (as opposed to simple rule-following). The idea and example of faith as the foundation of one's relationship with God is Abraham's great legacy.

The message of David's life is being "a man after God's own heart." Centuries later,

---

Life Message Indicators

1. **Soapbox Issues:** The ideals and issues you always talk about.
2. **Places of Power:** Where you have unusual authority and impact.
3. **Qualification:** What you've been through makes people listen to you.
4. **Drawing:** Where you are drawn to others and they're drawn to you.

David's life story still communicates the full range of what it means to be human. His story and Psalms convey that heart-level dialog with his God as his legacy to us.

The primary message of your life always comes through progressive revelation, because it is progressively built into your heart over years of life experience. Even in the instances where God revealed a life message from the beginning (as with David and Abraham), it was not until much later in life that they understood, embodied and lived it. So don't worry if you aren't totally clear on what the message of your life is—God knows, and He is working every detail of your life to bring it to fullness in you.

Calling Lifestyles

A final aspect of incarnation has to do with lifestyle. There is a life pattern—including your standard of living, the things you choose to own and the schedule you keep—that is most congruent with your message. This *Lifestyle of Your Calling* (14.6) can greatly reinforce the power of the message God has placed in you or it can be a great hindrance to it.

Jesus clearly understood that He was to live a lifestyle that fit his call. For example:

- "The foxes have holes and the birds of the air have nests, but the Son of Man has nowhere to lay His head" (Mt. 8:20).

- "The son of man did not come to be served, but to serve, and give his life as a ransom for many" (Mt. 20:28).

- "…though He was rich, yet for your sake He became poor, so that you through His poverty might become rich" (II Cor. 8:9).

- "The Son of Man has come eating and drinking, and you say, 'Behold, a gluttonous man and a drunkard, a friend of tax collectors and sinners!'" (Luke 7:34).

- "… they were amazed that He had been speaking with a woman, yet no one said, 'What do you seek?' or, 'Why do you speak with her?'" (John 4:27)

If Jesus had preferred to stay in the villas of the upper crust of society instead of with the working class, or had owned slaves on a big estate in the hills of Galilee, or even lived the ascetic life of a Pharisee, His lifestyle would have undermined His message. The son of man came to seek and save the lost—and that mission required Him to live among them, as one of them. That's why He chose to go to their parties, to hang out with people who drank, to break the gender and culture barriers by talking to a Samaritan woman. All His lifestyle choices—from money to social customs to the circles He ran in—reinforced His message.

There is a unique lifestyle that fully supports your Calling. If you are called to offer hospitality in your home and reach professional people, your Calling lifestyle may include an exquisitely decorated house with which to do it. Another's call may mean buying whatever house is closest to a college campus and taking in students as boarders, or finding a dilapidated crack house and renovating it as a place to reach unwed mothers in a poor neighborhood. For all of these situations, only one particular kind of house will do—any of the others would be an obstacle to the call.

Take half an hour in a quiet place and reflect back on your life story. We're going to identify the major shaping events in your life and what they mean for your destiny.

Step 1: Identify Shaping Events

In the left hand column, record major transitions, difficult experiences, important relational influences—the experiences in life that most deeply shaped who you are. Times you met God in tough circumstances and were transformed are particularly likely to produce life messages.

Step 2: Discover Life Messages from Events

Take each experience in turn, and reflect and journal on it using these questions:

- How did this experience shape who I am? How am I a different person because I went through it?

- How did I meet God in this? How did God use it to shape my character?

- What is the message this experience built into me for others? Where am I drawn to others, qualified to speak to them, and have a deep impact because of this experience?

Shaping Event	Life Message

Life Messages in Action

An alternate way to discover life messages is to find the places where they operate in your life now, and then work backwards to discover where they came from.

Step 1: Examine Your Life

Take a look at the following four areas to try to identify your life messages in action. Jot down your responses to the questions on a blank sheet of paper.

- **Soapbox Issues:** What are the themes you come back to over and over when you are helping or serving others? What are you always talking passionately about? What do you most yearn to impart to people?

- **Impact:** Where are your places of greatest impact? What do you seem to impart to other people there? What messages do they consistently learn or draw from you?

- **Qualification:** Are there situations you can speak into because of what you've been through, where others can't? Where have you met God in suffering in a way that opens the door to other's hearts? What is the message you have for people in that situation?

- **Drawing:** What people are you most drawn to help? Who is drawn to you? What are they looking for, and what do you most want them to receive from you?

Step 2: What Messages Stand Out?

When you've been through all the questions, step back and look over what you jotted down. What messages come out the strongest? Are there themes that are repeated over several of your entries? These themes are your life message candidates.

Step 3: Where Did it Come from?

Take a few moments and trace back each potential message to where it came from. How was this idea implanted in you? Was there a certain experience or relationship that imprinted this message on your heart? True life messages always have a component of meeting God in a significant way in their origin, because the message is something God plants in your heart.

Step 4: Name and Record

If you haven't done so already, name your message. A single word, a pithy phrase or a fragment of Scripture can be perfect—make it something memorable that sticks with you. And write down the story of how that message developed in your life! These stories are some of your most powerful tools for impacting others—so don't let the memory fade.

If something is a true life message, the people who are close to you will know it (probably because they've heard you talk about it or seen it in your life repeatedly). For confirmation, find a friend, fellow leader or family member, and ask for some honest feedback on your tentative life message list. Describe the self-discovery process you are going through and explain what life messages are before you start. Here are some life message symptoms:

- Jesus is readily apparent in your life here.
- You paid a price for that incarnation.
- It's a theme you return to repeatedly.
- You have unusual impact on others in this area.
- Others are drawn to you for help and solace here.

For Feedback

If you want feedback on a list of possible life messages that you've already developed, try this approach:

- "I've tentatively identified ____ as a life message—an area where there's a God-implanted message in my heart to pass on to others. What do you think? Do you see that in me? Are the life message symptoms apparent here?"
- "Which of the items on this list do you most see as my life messages?"
- "Help me understand what makes you say that. What specific examples in my life lead you to that conclusion?"

For Input

If you've had a hard time identifying life messages on your own and you'd like some input from those around you, use the following questions.

- "What do you think my life messages might be?"
- "Where do you see me operate with unusual impact? What is the heart of that impact?"
- "When I am serving, when do I most connect with others at the heart level? What is the message I communicate in those times?"
- "Can you help me understand what makes you say that? What specific examples in my life story make you believe that?"

You may also want to show your friend the *Life Messages in Action* exercise (14.2) and talk through some of the questions there together.

The Message of Your Life

The *Message of Your Life* is the heart of your call—the key way the heart of Christ touches the people you love and serve. Here are several ways to get at that central message. This is an exercise that you'll come back to repeatedly as God unfolds more and more of his purpose to you. So do it in pencil, and don't worry about getting it perfect the first time. You can use any one or all of the approaches below.

Option 1: Start with Life Messages

Look over the list of your life messages from exercise 14.1. Use the questions below or work with your coach to identify a dominant message or a theme in your messages:

- Is there one dominant message?
- If the people you serve really "got" only one message, which would you want it to be?
- Where do all your messages point? Is there a theme they converge around?

Option 2: Start from Your Life Mission

Take your *Life Mission* (15.4) and explore why you want to do it:

- What does doing this communicate or give to people that is vitally important to you?
- Why does God care about you doing this? How does it reveal His heart?
- What's the central message God wants to touch people with through your task?

Option 3: Revisit Your Passions

Go back to the work you did on your Passions (see chapters 7-10), and examine it for clues to your message:

- What have your life experiences made you most passionate about communicating or giving to others?
- Which of your passions are closest to the *Passion Bull's Eye* (7.1)? What value is most important to you? What's the message in it?
- If your legacy was that five people fully caught your passion and carried it on after you were gone, what would you most want them to catch from you?

Part II: Create a Statement

Once you've looked at the options above, take your message and distill it down to a sentence. You may need several tries or to let it stew for a while before you come up with something you really like. Don't worry—that's normal.

Life Messages (14.1)

Life Mission (15.5)

Passions

The Message of My Life: Statement

Calling through Suffering

This exercise offers a series of questions to help you uncover life messages or callings that are connected somehow with suffering. Take some time to meditate on each question, or (especially if you are an extrovert!) talk it through with a good friend or spouse. What surfaces as you ponder these questions? What do these experiences have to say about what you may be called to do?

- What are your most significant experiences of suffering?
- What does this make you passionate about changing?

Confrontation

- What injustice makes you want to rise up and fight for the good of all?
- What's the injustice you see, where you also have a compelling vision of the better future that could be?

Prevention

- Where do you have a deep desire to save others from what you've suffered?
- What experiences sensitized you to that particular area?

Compassion

- What kinds of images or situations consistently cause compassion to rise up in you?
- Where do you identify with the weak or the needy? Who are the people your heart is drawn to, and why?

Qualification

- What difficult experiences give you a platform to speak to others in that same area?
- Who will listen to you because of what you've been through, that would never listen otherwise? What do you want to impart to them?

Overcoming

- Where have you overcome significant difficulty in your life?
- What have you done well that you are motivated to share with others?

Acceptance

- Where have you learned to walk in great peace in the midst of suffering or injustice?
- Where has God given you special grace to accept as a gift something others might see as a curse?

We all have a lifestyle that fits what we were created to do and be. What you own, how you spend your money and your time, where you live—all these things have implications for your destiny. Start with the picture you created in the *Ideal Lifestyle* exercise (8.3). Then add lifestyle elements that directly support fulfilling your God-given call using the questions below.

Identification

Jesus became one of us so that we could approach God through His life. How must you identify with the audience you are called to serve (live their lifestyle) so you can understand them and they can approach you?

Qualification

What life experience will qualify you to speak to your target group? What kind of track record, life story or lifestyle would open the doors to their hearts? What life would make you "real" to them, and what would make you look like a hypocrite?

Standard of Living

What standard of living are you called to? (It should be determined by the needs of your calling, not by rising to meet whatever income you can generate!) What possessions are needed for your call and what would be a distraction or distance you from your audience? What kind of home, wardrobe, income, hobbies, etc. would fit best with your life mission?

Location

Where do you need to live or spend your time to walk in your call? What lifestyle would get you into the lives of your target audience and support you best as you pursue your mission?

Fellowship

Who do you need to be with to fulfill your destiny? What kind of lifestyle will put you in the relationships and the teams you need around you? What community will best support you in what you are called to do and be?

Chapter 15: Calling/ Audience, Task and Impact

"The end point of our best desires is not selfish, not the having of love and belonging, but the giving of it."

Peter Temes, in *The Power of Purpose*

"So, Nate—give me some specific examples. What kind of people are you most drawn to help?"

"I guess it would be other parents, people with teenagers—that sort of thing."

"What draws you to them?"

"Well, we had so much of a struggle with Jennifer that I guess we feel for them. And when Jeremy came along, it was a whole different set of issues. So we look around at church and in the neighborhood, and when we see the kids acting out or the parents yelling across the street at them in frustration, we want to do something."

"Let's get a bit more specific here. If you could name one person or couple who exemplify the kind of parents you want to reach, who would it be?"

"Hmm… Maybe Jeff and Emily down the street? They've got two in junior high and one in high school."

"Tell me more—why them?"

"We talk every so often when I see him jogging. I can tell they're hurting. The middle one, Brendan, barely talks to them. They just don't know how to bridge the gap."

"What else?"

"Part of the reason I picked them is because we have some natural contact—I run into them and I see their kids around, so I have some idea of what's going on. But mostly I see the little things they don't know how to do that would make all the difference. Like going to their soccer games—Jeff is always too busy, but he doesn't even connect his absence with what's going on with his kids."

"So I heard four things that draw you to Jeff and Emily: kids in their teens, people in proximity to you that you see in your daily routine; the little parenting skills that they are missing, and the hurt you see in them over the communication gap. Anything else?"

"Well… Jeff's a professional guy like me, so we have something in common. And Emily and Charlene seem to hit it off. That's something important. We like to do this as a couple, so it is important that Charlene connects with the wife as well as me with the husband."

"Good. Anything about the kids other than being teenagers?"

"Well, obviously that they are troubled to a certain extent. I'm not really drawn to situations where the kids are doing fine—they don't need me—and kids with drug problems or abuse issues seem a bit out of my league. So probably your basic American parents who just don't quite know how to cope with their teenagers."

"That's a great description. Last time we were working on the message of your life—how does this target audience tie in with your message?"

"Oh—that connects the dots! My message is, 'There is a unique way for you in your situation, and God will show it to you if you make it job one to find it.' Even better would be, 'Every kid is unique, there is a unique way for a parent to touch that kid's heart, and you need to find that way.' These are the people I see every day who can't find their way—and that's who I want to help."

Calling is an external commission from God *for others.* That "for others" phrase has great significance for life purpose discovery. If your life purpose is for others, you're going to have to figure out who those "others" are, how you are going to serve them, and how you want to impact them. Those three things are your *Audience, Task* and *Impact.*

Your *Audience* is the people or need you are called to. You may serve whole people groups, a few individuals you know by name, or about anything in between. Or the call may focus on meeting a need in a way that impacts certain people. In this example, Nate felt called to reach certain people (couples with troubled teens) with specific needs (a parent's heart, which was Nate's life message) that were in a certain place (in

---

Your Audience Might Be…

- **Specific, Named Individuals**
  Like your kids or a young man you mentor.

- **A Group**
  People in your profession, the homeless in your community or your employees.

- **A Point of Contact**
  Like individuals you meet in your job, or those in your neighborhood or church.

- **People with a Certain Need**
  Like Down syndrome kids, villages in Sudan that need a well or shut-ins needing home maintenance help.

- **A Societal Need**
  You help society at large— like a researcher creating cancer drugs, or a forest ranger who cares for a national park.

proximity to his life). The coach brought out these details by using an *exemplar*—a real individual who personifies the qualities of Nate's target audience. The box on the previous page includes a list of possible types of audiences.

Ultimate Impact

Your *Impact* is the "why" of your call—the outcome it produces in others' lives (some call this your Legacy or Ultimate Contribution). It's why God commissioned you to do your life mission in the first place. Your ultimate contribution is not the doing of the calling task, but how that task and the message that comes through it changes lives.

Defining Calling as a Message to an Audience for an Impact may seem a little restrictive at first. Many professions are focused on creating tangible objects of value (like auto workers, artists or chefs) instead of directly helping people. How do those examples fit the model?

> ### Calling is:
>
> A ***message*** you embody
> To a specific ***audience***
> For an ultimate ***impact***
> Through a unique ***task.***

Actually, this focus on impact is a key distinctive of biblical life purpose. As Christians, we believe in a heaven so incredible that nothing you can have on earth has any value compared to being there. And people are eternal, but things are not. Therefore, *possessions and things only have true, eternal value as avenues for impacting people.* That's the point of the parable of the unrighteous steward: use whatever tangible things you have to invest in people now, so when things pass away those people will be there to welcome you into heaven.

The beauty of focusing on impact is that it isn't the job you have that matters—it's how your heart touches people as you do your job. A plumber can channel his own unique message of Christ through his job in the same way that a pastor can, by allowing Christ be in every act of service, every kind word to a customer and every worship song that wafts up from the crawl space where he's working. Even doing a dirty job with excellence and a great attitude is a message. And in a Kingdom where the last shall be first, there will be unknown plumbers who attain higher stature in heaven than some famous leaders.

Finding Your "One Thing?"

Your *Task* is the primary channel the Message of your life goes through in order to Impact your Audience. It's the wineskin of your call—the practical form your message takes on when it is communicated. While the method of fulfilling a call (the task) can change with changing circumstances, the message rooted in your core identity stays much the same.

Your vocation (i.e. your job) may be the primary channel for the unique message of Christ in your life. Or it may not. Tent-making missionaries, home-school moms, a worker on permanent disability or retirees are all examples of people whose calling task is not synonymous with a job.

This leads us to an important question: was your unique call ever meant to be channeled through only one particular role or task in the first place? The "City Slickers" movies starring Billy Crystal are a good example of this concept. The key line in the movie was "you have to find your 'one thing'"—that one unique role or accomplishment that is your purpose in life, that you must find and do.

Some individuals *are* called in this way. Their life mission is to build a certain organization, take a given leadership position or complete a visionary project. For people like Mother Teresa, Warren Buffet, John the Baptist or Abraham Lincoln, that "one thing" is obvious.

But does everyone have a "one thing?" I had a conversation a few weeks ago with a staff pastor in a large church. He was an engaging, 50's, self-confessed A.D.D. man who seemed very contented and energized by his role. When I asked him what he did, I discovered he was essentially the church's troubleshooter: whenever there was a difficult assignment or something new that needed to be launched, they called on him. And after three to six months of getting that project going, he would move to another role. He loved it: lots of variety, and the ability to get in there, quickly evaluate the situation, and then hand it off to others. His call was not to one particular accomplishment, but to serve in a certain way in a whole series of projects.

That's actually a pretty common Calling pattern. If your mission is to demonstrate the father heart of God to kids, you may express it through coaching little league, running for the school board, parenting, or joining the Big Brother program. Any of those can work. At the far end of the spectrum from the "one thing"

Your Life Task May Be...

1. A **single** project to complete or role to faithfully execute.

2. A whole **series** of projects or roles that all communicate your message.

3. A particular **service** done through many individual acts in many different roles and venues.

people are those whose call is simply to be who they are and do what they are good at in whatever opportunity happens to come their way that day. The myriads of faithful people who serve in the background fixing things, setting up chairs, attending to practical needs and keeping the world from falling apart often fit this pattern.

Who Do You Love?

One way to start finding your Audience is to look at the people you've already helped in your life. In the left column, jot down specific individual and groups you've helped in a significant way in the past. Briefly note how you served each one. Once you have the left column filled up, start looking for patterns or common elements. What types of people or needs consistently appear in your list? They may be a certain age, gender, nationality or socio-economic status; people with specific needs or that you bump into in certain places, neighbors, saved or unsaved, etc. What characterizes the people you help?

People & Groups I've Helped	Characteristics/Needs

This exercise offers three separate options for identifying your Audience.

Option 1: Start with Life Message

Your message points naturally to an audience that needs that message. Start with the *Life Messages* you identified (14.1), and try asking yourself the following questions:

- What kind of people are you drawn to because of this message? Who is drawn to this message in you?
- Who do you notice because of this message that others miss? What needs are you sensitized to?
- Who does this message or the experience behind it qualify you to serve?
- Who needs your message?

Option 2: Check Several Exercises

- What has God revealed about your audience? Review the *Revelation Journal* (13.2).
- Look back at Passion and Preparation. Who have you served with passion and impact? Who are you prepared to serve? Who do you dream about serving? *Destiny Events* (12.1), *Dreams* (8.1) and the *Passion Bull's Eye* (7.1) are great places to look.
- Add any info from the *Who Do You Love?* exercise (15.1).

Option 3: Exemplars

You may find it easiest to describe your audience if you think of a specific person you know. Who do you know that best exemplifies the people you want to touch? Then describe the qualities of that person or their need that make them your example. If you are a practical, down-to-earth thinker, this type of concrete picture of a real person may be the most helpful.

> **Your Audience Might Be...**
>
> - **Specific, Named Individuals**
>   Like your kids or a young man you mentor.
>
> - **A Group**
>   People in your profession, the homeless in your community or your employees.
>
> - **A Point of Contact**
>   Like individuals you meet in your job, or those in your neighborhood or church.
>
> - **People with a Certain Need**
>   Like Down syndrome kids, villages in Sudan that need a well or shut-ins needing home maintenance help.
>
> - **A Societal Need**
>   You help society at large—like a researcher creating cancer drugs, or a forest ranger who cares for a national park.

Part II: Name Your Audience

Finally, create a brief description of your audience. It can be a bullet list of qualities and needs, or a specific named group (i.e. Latino businesswomen in Bakersfield). Try to express it as succinctly as possible. Create a profile of what a typical person in your sweet spot would look like—their age, where they live, marital status, needs, what's on their mind, etc.

Name Your Audience

Your Ultimate Impact is the lasting effect your message has on your audience in the course of your life. You are called to serve for a reason—to create an ultimate impact. How do you want to change the lives of those around you?

Naming the Impact

Take the message you identified (see 14.4 or 14.1) and begin to think through how you see that message touching others. If you are having a hard time visualizing the impact you desire, identify your target audience first (15.1 and 15.2) and then come back to this exercise.

- How do you want to change their outward circumstances?
- How will your message touch their hearts?
- What suffering will you alleviate, or what blessing will you bring them?
- When the people around you remember you after you are gone, what do you most want them to say about how you impacted them?

Create an Exemplar

The exercise may become more real for you if you find an exemplar: a real person who is a near-perfect example of your audience. Find an exemplar with the *Audience for My Message* exercise (15.2). How would you answer the questions above for this specific person?

Life Mission/Calling Task

Your life mission is the task or role that best channels your Message to your Audience for a certain Impact.

Step 1: Review

Take 20 minutes or so to flip through all the work you've done on Passion, Design and Preparation. Make sure and look at big dreams (8.1) plus your Message (14.1 or 14.4), Audience (15.2) and Impact (15.3). As you review, reflect on the following questions and jot down whatever comes to mind:

- What do these insights tell me about the task(s) I am called to do in my life?
- What task(s) or roles am I drawn to and might be great channels for my message?
- What have I done in the past that conveys my message well, and what tasks and roles would let me do more of that?

Step 2: Task or Tasks?

Some individuals accomplish their call through a single role or life task, others through series of tasks that all display their message and still others by simply engaging in acts of kindness wherever life takes them on a given day. Are you called to one ultimate task, or a certain type of service done in many ways? If your call is to a series of smaller tasks, what theme would hold those things together?

Step 3: Create a Statement

Now, take your jottings and distill them down to a one-sentence statement. Simple and memorable is best! You may need to play with several versions or to let it stew for a while before you come up with something you really like.

Chapter 16: Calling/ The Convergent Role

"I went into the woods because I wished to live deliberately, to front only the essential facts of life, and see if I could not learn what it had to teach, and not, when I came to die, discover that I had not lived."

Henry David Thoreau

"I've had a good run these last 10 years", Brian stated in our first session, "But now I'm getting a little antsy. I'm 55 years old, and I can see the end of my productive life coming ahead of me. That creates an urgency to maximize my impact for the time I have left, and to make sure I leave a legacy behind."

Brian was a secure, mature leader in the fulfillment stage of his calling journey.[5] What he wanted was to craft a role that fit his message, mission and audience—and his Design. Over the next few months, we identified his type and his best strengths. Then we studied his current role. What was he doing that fit him well? What didn't fit, or wasn't a priority? Brian was more of a visionary than an implementer, so we talked about how he could rearrange staff roles to allow him to look at the future while others pushed out the day-to-day program. He found that some tasks he'd assumed would always be in his corner were things he could actually delegate. Others could be minimized by changing his focus or job description.

Understanding his own design opened up a new world of opportunities for his staff, too. As roles on the team were reconfigured, Brian aggressively worked to

---

5   See *The Calling Journey* for more on stages of calling.

discover their strengths and types, and to create roles that fit them. One key leader was clearly called to something larger and was chafing in his current role. It was hard to let go of his right-hand man, but Brian was able to help him identify what he needed and transition into a better-fitting role elsewhere.

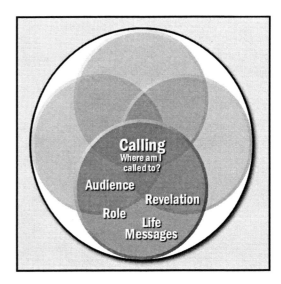

But it still wasn't enough. What began to rise to prominence in Brian was his urge to write, to mentor other leaders and to move into a larger sphere of influence. That put a whole new twist into working with his role. We began to explore other leadership models that would allow him to contribute his best at home but still have time to go on the road—like co-pastoring, moving into an apostolic relationship with his church, or raising up and gradually transitioning to a successor.

The whole process was very energizing for Brian. "This is great! I've been feeling like it's either stay here and be stuck with a bunch of stuff that isn't me and isn't my best, or leave everything and start over. This gives me a whole new way to think about fulfilling my call."

Your life task is the optimum channel for the message of your life. Sometimes (particularly for organizational leaders) the venue for that task is a certain convergent role. Other individuals express their call through multiple tasks and positions instead of one best-fit role. Before you start working on convergent roles, make sure you grasp this distinction (see pg. 139).

If you are a leader in the early stages of life, you are in training for your call.

> *A convergent role enables you to accomplish your life task through a role that fits your Design.*

It's less important what role you are in than what you are learning along the way. In your 20's, it's about accumulating the wide variety of experiences you need to help you sort out your call and prepare for it. In your 30's, roles should engage more of your strengths, but they won't necessarily be a perfect fit or even be in your area of call. In fact, sometimes God *removes* leaders in this stage from well-fitting roles to work on their hearts. It's not until your 40's or 50's, when you are at the stage of fulfilling your life mission, that creating a role that fits you to a tee is crucial. So assuming that you should strive to get into a convergent role no matter what your age is is not realistic.

Influence Style

One important part of creating a convergent role is learning your *Influence Style*. It's the method you use to get your message across. Every leader has a preferred influence style (take a few minutes and scan the list on 16.1), and aligning with it increases energy, effectiveness and satisfaction. Organizational leaders usually don't want to be practitioners—they are fine with someone else doing the hands-on work if they can build the team that does it. Leaders with a Second Man style prefer not to be the point person—they flourish best as the right-hand man to another leader.

Here's a real-life example. Frank's dream was to create an inner healing center where people could come for several-day stays in a retreat setting and receive ministry for inner wounds. After working at it for a while and not making much progress, I took a different tack. "Frank, let's stop and take a look at your influence style. That's your preferred method of functioning in leadership—the way that you impact people the best. Some people are organization builders: they create structures and teams that do the mission, while they lead the team. Some are trainers who teach others to do the ministry. Some are mentors who invest in a few others to carry on their legacy. And some are practitioners—they want to do the hands-on ministry themselves. Which one of those best fits you?"

Frank quickly identified that he was a practitioner. He felt most productive and in the zone when he was working one-on-one with a person in need of healing. The problem was that Frank's dream required him to function in an organization builder style—to envision, fund, build and maintain a retreat center where these people could stay. The breakthrough came when Frank realized he could take his healing center on the road instead of creating a physical location for it. Scaling down the organizational part of his vision and working through existing retreat centers could allow him to focus on the personal ministry he loved best. He could also do training (his second preferred influence style) through other ministries. The idea of not having any fund-raising or management duties lifted a big weight off of his shoulders.

Spheres of Influence

- Personal Relationships (a disciple or parent)
- Neighborhood, Church or Workplace
- Your Organization
- City/Locality (local leader)
- Profession (leading figure or influencer in your entire profession)
- Regional
- National
- International

Sphere of Influence

Another important question is your sphere of influence—the size of stage on which your destiny plays out. I like to break this question down into two parts: your *Immediate Sphere* and your *Ultimate Sphere*. Your immediate sphere is the size group that you like to work with at one time. Are you at your best working one-on-one, with small groups (up to 20), medium-size groups (under 150), or larger groups?

I'm a small group and one-on-one guy. My call is about personal transformation and reshaping identity, and those things don't happen very effectively in mass meetings. So I choose to work in smaller contexts. However, my ultimate sphere is much larger. I dream of influencing movements and creating models that many others employ. My materials are published in other countries, so even though I never travel internationally (except in Canada), my ultimate sphere of influence is international.

These two sphere questions make for interesting combinations. I have a pretty small immediate sphere but a very large ultimate one. A local pastor with a Trainer/Teacher influence style might have a large immediate sphere but a local ultimate one—while he preaches to large groups, it's pretty much the same local group every time. So you can have a large immediate sphere and a small ultimate one, or vice versa. None is intrinsically better than any other—the best one is the one God created you for.

One other variation of sphere is with legacy: the ongoing impact of your life after you are gone. An interesting example is St. Augustine's mother Monica. She was sainted for her role in praying her son into the Kingdom from an immoral, profligate lifestyle. Her immediate sphere of influence was basically one person; her ultimate sphere of influence was basically one person, but her legacy includes the impact of the people she impacted, caluculated over generations. Augustine is a giant figure in church history. So although Monica functioned in a very small sphere all her life, she created an enormous legacy. You never know what the final impact of your life will be!

Developing Your Convergent Role

Begin with the *Influence Style* exercise (16.2) to discover your preferred style. Worksheet 16.1 includes a list of 12 possible styles, along with a description of each one and its lasting legacy. If you like, you can explore your *Sphere of Influence* (16.3) as well. Then start working on a description of your convergent role with the *80/20 Job Description* (16.4).

You can do this in two ways. You can start with your current job and figure out how it would have to be modified to let you spend 80% of your time functioning out of your strengths. A great way to flesh this description out is to think back on other roles you've had over the years, and add elements from them that match your strengths, too. Or, if your current role isn't a good starting place, you can go back to your Passions and Design and create a role that fits you from scratch. Either way, strive for an ideal role, even if it seems unattainable right now. If you don't shoot for the best, you'll never know how close you could have come to it if you tried!

Here's a list of eleven common leadership influence styles with each one's legacy.

- **Organization Builder**: You exert influence through starting and building visionary organizations. Church planters and entrepreneurs fall in this category.
  Lasting Legacy: The impact of that organization both now and after you are gone.

- **Organizational Leader**: You lead within existing organizations, and your influence comes through the organization accomplishing its collective mission.
  Lasting Legacy: What's accomplished by the organization through your contributions.

- **Second Man:** Your greatest influence is serving as the right hand of a large-sphere leader. Alone, your influence is small, but in partnership you soar.
  Lasting Legacy: Your own impact plus the impact of the leader/ministry you served.

- **Service:** You influence through practical service or doing tasks for others. You're the person who does the hands-on work that makes a vision happen.
  Lasting Legacy: A part in the influence of every person and project your served.

- **Networking:** Your influence comes through connecting people and opportunities through a peer network. Your impact is through how much more is accomplished by bringing people together than is by them working alone.
  Lasting Legacy: The fruit borne by those connections and opportunities.

- **Ideation:** Sharing your original ideas is what gives you influence. Your best contribution is thinking and communicating those thoughts to others through writing, speaking or media.
  Lasting Legacy: The impact of those ideas and every person or project they touch.

- **Family:** Your primary influence and legacy is through your children and what you have invested in them as a parent, discipler and friend.
  Lasting Legacy: Children that surpass you, and whoever is served through them.

- **Mentor/Discipler**: Your greatest impact is on the people whose lives you have changed by walking with them one-on-one, and their lives are your legacy.
  Lasting Legacy: A cadre of disciples who carry on your message after you are gone.

- **Trainer/Teacher:** Your best impact comes through imparting skills, wisdom and knowledge to groups using your communication abilities.
  Lasting Legacy: The changed lives of your pupils and those they touch because of you.

- **Practitioner**: You want to do hands on-ministry instead of organizing, training or empowering others to do it. Your role must keep you in direct contact with the people you serve.
  Lasting Legacy: The lives of the people you help and those they touch because of you.

- **Empowerer:** Your influence comes by promoting, encouraging and believing in other leaders.
  Lasting Legacy: What those leaders accomplish because of your sponsorship.

Your Influence Style

Every leader prefers certain methods of exerting influence. Influence styles are particular channels your calling runs through best. Knowing your style is very helpful in crafting a role that fits your Design.

Step 1: Find Your Style

From the list of common leadership influence styles in 16.1, choose the two that best fit you (or make up your own if none really fit).

Step 2: Apply Your Style

Take a role or dream you are pursuing and evaluate it in light of your preferred style:

- What percentage of your time would you get to spend in your preferred influence modes in this role?
- What are the major tasks or responsibilities in this role that would require you to function outside of your best influence styles?
- What are three creative ways you could reconfigure this role to increase the amount of time you spent in your preferred influence style?

On what playing field you are called to exert influence? Your calling may be to thoroughly and deeply mentor six people in your lifetime—or to influence whole organizations, professions or even nations. Bigger spheres are not necessarily better—the best sphere for you is the one God made you for. This exercise looks at two types of spheres.

Part I: Your Immediate Sphere

Your immediate sphere of influence has to do with the size group you feel you are at your best working with at any one time. Do you influence others most effectively one-on-one, in a small group or team (under 20), in medium groups (under 150) or large groups? Remember, this is about influence. Think of a number of situations where you were very effective in exerting a positive influence. Which size sphere works best for you?

Part II: Your Ultimate Sphere

Your ultimate sphere of influence is the sum total of the influence of your lifetime. You may touch thousands of people only once or twice through brief, chance encounters, books or speaking engagements. Or you may spend years with family, neighbors or a few others, and sow very deeply into the lives of only a few. Here are some questions to get you thinking:

- Do you best influence through long-term relationships or one-time encounters?
- Do you prefer to go deep with a few or briefly touch many?
- Is your influence direct and person-to-person, or through indirect means such as ideas, corporate cultures, training others or organizations you are part of?
- What is the ultimate task you want to accomplish in life? On what size of stage will that mission play out?
- What spheres (business or ministry, a certain profession or organization, a certain locale) will your influence ultimately touch?

The 80/20 Job Description  16.4

The 80/20 rule says you should spend 80% of your time in the area of your gifts and strengths—but that most people spend 80% of their time on things they aren't good at! Thinking through a role that fits is an important part of succeeding as a leader.

Part I: Assessing the Current Role

Think of the kind of tasks and responsibilities your role requires. In the left hand column, jot down the ones you are best at and find energizing. In the right hand column, list tasks or responsibilities that aren't your strengths, you find draining or you'd love to delegate if you could. Review your *Strengths* and *Weaknesses* inventories (7.2 and 7.3), influence style and your personality type report to add to your lists.

What Fits Me	What Doesn't Fit

16.4 The 80/20 Job Description

Part II: The 80/20 Job Description

Now, create a job description for yourself that lets you spend 80% of your time doing what you do best: the things in the left column above. The idea here is to define your absolute best. Let yourself dream freely about where you want to be in three years and push the boundaries of what seems attainable—just bypass any obstacles in your current circumstances. You may find it helpful to look back at jobs you've had in the past and take the parts of each one you really liked to make up your dream job.

- What kind of role would best support me functioning in my life task?
- What's my average day/week look like in this ideal role?
- In what strength areas am I spending 80% of my time? What am I delegating that is not my strength?
- What job description would maximize my ability to do what's in the left column above and minimize the time I spend on the right?

Part III: Realigning Your Role

Once you've defined your ideal, you can begin moving toward it. Compare your ideal to your current role and note the differences. Then choose the three places where you could most easily transition toward your ideal (the quick wins) and work with your coach to create strategies for changing each one.

Chapter 17: Life Purpose Summaries

There is a tide in the affairs of men,
Which taken at the flood, leads on to
fortune; omitted, all the voyage of their life
is bound in shallows and in miseries.
On such a full sea we are now afloat;
And we must take the current when it serves,
or lose our ventures.

William Shakespeare, in *Julius Caesar*

The final step in the life purpose discovery process is bringing all your insights together in a set of brief summary statements. Life purpose statements clarify the core of your call and put it in a memorable form. There is great utility in a memorized one-sentence purpose statement you can call up at a moment's notice.

The *Workbook* provides a two-page *Life Purpose Summary* worksheet (17.2) for those key life purpose statements. In this compact format it can easily be copied and put up on the wall—a great way to keep your values, vision, mission and message in front of you. The worksheet is also available as a free electronic download at www. ALeadersLifePurpose.com.

If you've completed the first-level exercises in the *Workbook*, you are already well on your way to having these summary statements completed. *Value Statements* (10.6) summarize the area of Passion. Personality type (from an assessment) provides a brief, memorable statement of your Design. Under Calling, the *Message of Your Life* and *Life Mission* exercises (14.4 and 15.5) produce being and doing summary statements that can be dropped right into the worksheet.

Those last two also provide a great way to create an overall *Life Purpose Statement* (17.3). Use the Message > Audience > Task > Impact format, and simply fill in all four to create your statement.

Here's an example. I serve on the board of a non-profit that provides leadership coaching to missionaries. Our aim is to help missionaries and mission organizations accomplish their objectives by increasing the health and effectiveness of the missionaries we coach. So a Calling statement for our organization might look like the first example on worksheet 17.1.

One other important piece of the puzzle is a *Life Vision Statement* (17.2). A vision statement is a visual picture of what it would look like to be fully living out your call. This summary is around a page in length. The focus is on capturing the feel of that future and connecting with the motivation of seeing your greatest Passion coming to fruition.

Several exercises can feed into this process, depending on what you have done to this point. You can draw on your work with envisioning a fun *Dream Lifestyle* (8.3), your *Ideal Team* (6.3) and the more serious *Lifestyle of Your Call* (14.6). Insights from the *80/20 Job Description* (16.4) about the convergent role should be fed in as well.

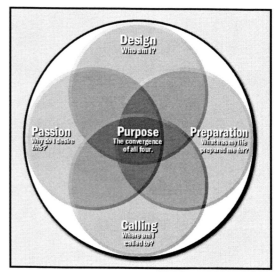

Where Do We Go from Here?

You're done! Now that you have a good picture of what you are supposed to do and be in life, how do you make use of it? Here are three places to start. The first is to simply set a short-term goal or two for moving toward that future, and begin pursuing it. Get yourself moving, right now, while you are feeling energized by the discovery process. If you don't do anything to convert your insights into action in the next two or three weeks, you probably won't act in the next two or three years, either.

Second, one of the biggest reasons leaders fail to fulfill their destiny is the lack of support structures in their lives. Support structures are things like boundaries, peer accountability, being in a small group, etc. Who and what is there to keep you on course with your life goals when you feel like giving up? For instance, life coaches can be a great aid in pursuing your life purpose. Their expertise, encouragement and understanding of how to turn dreams into actions can propel you forward much faster than you can on your own. If that's not available, find a peer, start meeting regularly, and hold each other accountable to take the steps that you choose.

A third step would be to read *The Calling Journey*. How you go about pursuing your life purpose is highly dependent on the Calling stage you are in. This book helps you understand the developmental process and what God wants to do in you in the life season you are in.

So go out and live the message you were made to be through the mission you were born to do! The world is waiting for the unique part only you can play.

Life Purpose Statement Examples

A Life Purpose Statement sums up your purpose in a single sentence. Here are a few examples. Notice that the order of the phrases (Message, Audience, Task and Impact) can be shuffled to make the statement read more smoothly.

Our purpose is to...

Demonstrate God's heart to empower, resource and care for	Message
Missionaries and mission organizations	Audience
Through providing leadership coaching	Task
In order to help them accomplish the Great Commission.	Impact

I am called to...

Embody the undeserved grace of God	Message
To unwed mothers,	Audience
To bring them into the family of God	Impact
By taking them in, caring for their children and helping them build a life.	Task

The words "embody" and "demonstrate" in the first lines build the being focus explicitly into the statement. This is what makes it a statement of your life purpose (both being and doing) and not just a life mission or task statement.

Here's an example of how to build a purpose statement from the individual exercises. If the *Message of Your Life* (14.4) is, "You can engage God from the heart in every circumstance, especially suffering and adversity, and be transformed"; and your *Life Mission* (15.4) is, "Building leadership character and developing systems that build leadership character"; a final life purpose statement might be:

I am called to...

Embody engaging God in every circumstance	*Message*
To build ministry leaders	*Audience*
Who are transformed to transform others	*Impact*
Through building systems that build leadership character.	*Task*

If you want to get fancy, you can add your *Sphere of Influence* (16.3) and *Influence Style* (16.2):

I embody engaging God in every circumstance	*Message*
To help ministry leaders worldwide	*Audience, Sphere*
Experience transformed character	*Impact*
Through prototyping and multiplying	*Influence Style*
Systems that build leadership character.	*Task*

LIFE MESSAGE

LIFE MISSION

TYPE

LIFE PURPOSE STATEMENT

LIFE VERSE

CORE VALUES

My Life Purpose

LIFE VISION STATEMENT

My Life Vision

Use the worksheet on the preceding pages to summarize your life purpose. This worksheet was designed for you to copy and put it up on the wall in a place where you see your purpose statements regularly. (The worksheet can also be downloaded as an electronic file from www.ALeadersLifePurpose.com so you can type your statements into it.) Feel free to do this exercise in pencil if you want to allow the freedom to go back and adjust your statements in the future.

The Message of My Life (14.4)

Transfer the statement you developed in exercise 14.4 to this blank.

Life Mission (15.4)

Write your one-sentence *Life Mission/Calling Task* statement (15.4) here.

Personality Type

Enter your personality type, StrengthsFinder© type or spiritual gifts here.

Life Purpose Statement (17.3)

Create a life purpose exercise using exercise 17.3 and insert it here. Put this one in big letters—it's the center of everything!

Life Verse

If you have a life verse, write it here. A life verse has special meaning, speaks about the direction of your life or the core of your being, and is one you return to again and again (you may have recorded it in exercise 13.2, the *Revelation Journal*).

Life Values (10.6)

Write in your short-phrase value statements from exercise 10.6 here. Values are a key part of making great decisions, so keeping them in front of you is a big plus.

Life Vision

A vision statement is a *visual picture* of what it would look like to be fully living out your call. You can draw on your work from several exercises: with envisioning a fun *Ideal Lifestyle* (8.3), your *Ideal Team* (6.3) and the more serious *Lifestyle of Your Call* (14.6). Insights from the *80/20 Job Description* (16.4) about your convergent role should also be included.

Since this is a vision exercise, it is important to include specific details. Statements like "I'll be living in Texas" or "I'll work with kids" are too vague. Where in Texas? What will your house look like? Your commute? Your neighborhood? If you are having a tough time being specific, walk yourself through an actual, specific day when you are living out your call.

The idea here is capturing the feel of that future, not about getting every detail perfect. So dream, enjoy the process and don't worry too much about whether it will all turn out exactly like this. Shoot for about a page of description.

Life Purpose Statement

An easy way to create a calling statement is to start with the Message (14.4), Impact (15.3), Audience (15.1) and Task (15.4) framework. Take a short phrase for each, and weave them together into a statement. The best statements are short, memorable, and uniquely you. Feel free to try different wordings or put the phrases in different order to get something that sounds right. Several examples of statements are provided in worksheet 17.1.

A life purpose statement is something you'll want to refer back to over and over, so keep it brief and to the point. One sentence is the goal. It is better to have short and memorable phrases you can unpack than a rambling, all-inclusive statement you can never bring to mind.

Your statement should include both your call to *be* the message and to *do* a task. That's why a word like "embody," "incarnate," "live out" or "demonstrate" is included in the first line. Here are some possible formats:

To embody my **Life Message**

to my **Audience**

through a **Role** or **Task** that fits me

for a certain **Impact**.

Or change the order of the phrases:

To live out my **Life Message**

through a **Task**

for a certain **Impact**

on my **Audience**.

You can also try this:

My God-given **Passion**

Serving those God draws to me (my **Audience**)

Through my strengths, gifts and abilities (**Design**)

Below are a few examples of additional coaching resources from Tony Stoltzfus, available through Coach22.com or your coaching retailer.

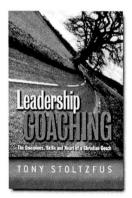

Leadership Coaching

As a complete overview of the fundamental skills and practices of coaching, *Leadership Coaching* is a great companion to this volume. The book features an introduction to the coaching model, a look at the value system and change theory underlying this approach, and a series of "Master Class" chapters that walk you through the basics of listening, asking, building support systems and more. Widely used as a basic coaching text, this book provides the tools you need to put life purpose insights in action.

The Master Coach Series

Each of these three CDs includes an hour of input and live coaching demos on a significant coaching skill. The first disc, *Problem Solving*, covers a variety of approaches used to generate options and creative solutions without telling the client what to do. *Changing Perspective* focuses on reframing techniques that break the client out of a limited viewpoint to look at life situations in new ways. *Coaching Visionaries* focuses on techniques used to clarify, refine and test a visionary idea or calling.

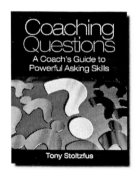

Coaching Questions

This best-selling coaching reference combines dozens of practical asking tools with over 1,000 examples of powerful coaching questions. Each major area of the coaching conversation is illustrated with multiple approaches. Covering everything from options and actions to decision-making strategies and reframing techniques, this book can help everyone from experienced coaches to trainees improve their asking proficiency.

Coaching Transitions

Life goes in cycles—from seasons where the focus is outward productivity to times of inward retooling. In this two-disc set, Tony discusses how our lack of understanding of transition causes us to try to escape these seemingly dry seasons instead of being transformed by them. Interwoven into the input is a full length coaching session and two interviews with former coaching clients who discuss their own transitional experiences and how they found and embraced purpose within their transitions.